Proverbs' Portraits The Men God Mentions

Joshua Rhoades

Published by Joshua Paul Rhoades, 2024.

While every precaution has been taken in the preparation of this book, the publisher assumes no responsibility for errors or omissions, or for damages resulting from the use of the information contained herein.

PROVERBS' PORTRAITS THE MEN GOD MENTIONS

First edition. September 2, 2024.

Copyright © 2024 Joshua Rhoades.

ISBN: 979-8227885036

Written by Joshua Rhoades.

Also by Joshua Rhoades

Courage Under Fire: David's Stand On The Battlefield
Jonah's Journey: Voices Of Redemption And Lessons In Obedience
The Furnace Of Faith: 12 Principles From The Heat Of Faith
Whispers of Hope: Inspiring Stories of Men's Prayers In Scripture
Frontier Legends: The Oregon Dream
Elijah: A Beacon Of Boldness
HOOK, LINE & SAVIOUR - Faith Reflections from Fishing
Driven By Faith: Motor Racing Inspired Christian Life
30 Day Devotional - Bold and Strong- Coffee Devotions for a
Courageous Christian Walk
Authentic Christianity: The Heart of Old Time Religion
Consider The Ant - God's Tiny Preachers
Flee Fornication: The Plea For Purity
Renewed Hope- How to Find Encouragement in God
Sounding The Call - The Voice of Conviction
The Altar - Where Heaven Meets Earth
The Bible's Battlefields- Timeless Lessons from Ancient Wars
The Sacred Art of Silence - How Silence Speaks in Scripture
Under Fire- The Sanctity of the Traditional Biblical Home
Who Is on the Lord's Side? A Call to Righteousness
What Is Truth? - From Skepticism to Submission
First and Goal- Faith and Football Fundamentals
From Dugout to Devotion- Spiritual Lessons from Baseball
Par for the Course- Faith and Fairways
The Believer's Pace- Tools for Running Life's Marathon

The Immutable Fortress- Security in God's Unchanging Nature
Biblical Bravery
Deer Stands and Devotions: A Hunter's Walk with God
Jesus Knows- Our Hearts, Our Responsibility
Restoration - Setting The Bone
Spiritual 911- God's Word for Life's Emergency's
The Freedom of Forgiveness
The Jezebel Effect - Ancient Manipulations Modern Lessons
The Shout That Stopped The Saviour
The Time Machine Chronicles: Old Testament Characters
Anchored In Truth Exploring The Depths of Psalm 119
Biblical Counsel on Anger
Proverbs' Portraits The Men God Mentions
Stumbling in the Dark - The Dangers of Alcohol

Introduction

In "Proverbs' Portraits - The Men God Mentions", we embark on a journey through the book of Proverbs, uncovering the different types of men that God highlights within its wisdom-filled pages. Proverbs, known for its practical advice and deep insights into human character, paints vivid pictures of the various ways men choose to live their lives. Some are wise and righteous, walking in the fear of the Lord and reaping the blessings of their faithfulness. Others are foolish, choosing paths of pride, laziness, deceit, and destruction that lead to their downfall. This book examines these contrasting portraits to provide readers with clear lessons that are as relevant today as they were when Proverbs was first written. We will explore the qualities that define a wise man—his humility, diligence, and integrity—and compare them to those of the foolish man, who is driven by pride, anger, and selfish desires. Through these examples, we learn not just about the consequences of their actions but also about the kind of character God values and the type of person He calls each of us to be. By studying the men God mentions in Proverbs, we gain insights that can shape our own lives, guiding us toward wisdom and away from folly. This book is not just an exploration of ancient texts but a practical guide for living a life that honors God. Whether you are seeking to grow in your own spiritual journey or help others along the way, "Proverbs' Portraits - The Men God Mentions" offers timeless truths that will encourage, challenge, and inspire you to live with wisdom and integrity to the honor and glory of God.

Chapter 1 – The Wise Man

Proverbs 1:5, "A wise man will hear, and will increase learning; and a man of understanding shall attain unto wise counsels," Proverbs 9:9, "Give instruction to a wise man, and he will be yet wiser: teach a just man, and he will increase in learning," and Proverbs 10:8, "The wise in heart will receive commandments: but a prating fool shall fall," provide a profound portrait of the wise man as described in the book of Proverbs. The wise man is characterized by his continuous pursuit of knowledge, his humility in accepting instruction, and his willingness to apply wisdom in his daily life. Unlike those who are foolish and reject guidance, the wise man recognizes the value of learning and grows wiser as he embraces instruction. His life is a testament to the importance of seeking wisdom, understanding the Lord's teachings, and living according to God's commandments. The lessons one can learn from the wise man in Proverbs are invaluable in our walk with the Lord, as they guide us to live a life that honors God, fosters spiritual growth, and leads to a deeper relationship with Him.

Proverbs 1:5 emphasizes the wise man's desire to listen and learn. "A wise man will hear, and will increase learning; and a man of understanding shall attain unto wise counsels." This verse teaches us that wisdom begins with the ability to listen—both to the Word of God and to the wise counsel of others. The wise man is not content with his current level of knowledge; he continually seeks to grow in understanding, knowing that there is always more to learn, especially in his relationship with God. In our walk with the Lord, this teaches us the importance of being open to learning from the Bible, from sermons, from fellow believers, and from life experiences. Just as the wise man values learning and is eager to receive instruction, we too should be willing to listen to God's voice and seek His wisdom in all aspects of our lives. This humility in learning is key to spiritual growth, as it allows us to deepen our understanding of God's will and apply it in our daily lives.

Proverbs 9:9 further illustrates the nature of the wise man by showing how he responds to instruction. "Give instruction to a wise man, and he will be yet wiser: teach a just man, and he will increase in learning." The wise man is not defensive or prideful when given advice or correction; instead, he embraces it as an opportunity to grow. This willingness to accept instruction and grow wiser is a crucial lesson for our walk with the Lord. It reminds us that we must be teachable and open to the guidance that God provides, whether through His Word, the prompting of the Holy Spirit, or the counsel of others. The wise man's eagerness to increase in learning is a model for how we should approach our faith journey—with a desire to continually grow in our knowledge of God and His ways. As we seek to become wiser in our spiritual lives, we should embrace every opportunity to learn and be instructed, understanding that each lesson brings us closer to the fullness of God's wisdom.

Proverbs 10:8 highlights the practical aspect of wisdom by emphasizing obedience to God's commandments. "The wise in heart will receive commandments: but a prating fool shall fall." The wise man is not just a hearer of the Word but a doer as well. He receives God's commandments with an open heart and applies them in his life, demonstrating his wisdom through his actions. This is a powerful lesson for our walk with the Lord, as it teaches us that true wisdom is not merely about acquiring knowledge but about living out that knowledge in obedience to God. The wise man's heart is aligned with God's will, and he shows his wisdom by following the path that God has set before him. In our own lives, this means that we must not only seek to understand God's teachings but also strive to live according to them. Obedience to God's commandments is a reflection of our wisdom and our commitment to following Him faithfully.

The wise man's life, as described in these proverbs, serves as a blueprint for how we should live as followers of Christ. His continuous pursuit of wisdom, his humility in receiving instruction, and his obedience to God's commandments are qualities that we should all strive to emulate. In our walk with the Lord, these qualities will help us to grow spiritually, to make decisions that honor God, and to build a life that is grounded in faith and wisdom. The wise man teaches us that wisdom is not a static quality but a dynamic process of learning, growing, and applying God's truths in our lives. As we seek to become wise in our own spiritual journey, we can look to the wise man of Proverbs as a model, remembering that wisdom is a gift from God that we must continually seek, nurture, and live out.

In conclusion, the wise man in Proverbs 1:5, 9:9, and 10:8 provides us with valuable lessons that are essential for our walk with the Lord. His example teaches us the importance of being eager to learn, open to instruction, and committed to obeying God's commandments. By following these principles, we can grow in wisdom and deepen our relationship with God, living a life that reflects His love, grace, and truth. The wise man's life is a reminder that true wisdom comes from God and that it is through our humility, teachability, and obedience that we can walk faithfully with the Lord and experience the fullness of His blessings.

Chapter 2 – The Foolish Man

Proverbs 1:7, "The fear of the Lord is the beginning of knowledge: but fools despise wisdom and instruction," Proverbs 12:15, "The way of a fool is right in his own eyes: but he that hearkeneth unto counsel is wise," and Proverbs 14:16, "A wise man feareth, and departeth from evil: but the fool rageth, and is confident," provide a powerful and cautionary depiction of the foolish man, or fool, as described in the book of Proverbs. The foolish man is characterized by his rejection of wisdom, his stubbornness in holding to his own flawed understanding, and his reckless confidence in the face of danger and wrongdoing. Unlike the wise man, who seeks knowledge, listens to counsel, and walks in the fear of the Lord, the fool is driven by pride, arrogance, and a disdain for instruction. The fool's life, as illustrated in these verses, serves as a warning against the dangers of rejecting God's wisdom and living according to one's own misguided perspective. The lessons one can learn from the foolish man in Proverbs are crucial for our walk with the Lord, as they teach us the importance of humility, the value of seeking wisdom, and the necessity of living in reverence to God. Proverbs 1:7 sets the foundation for understanding the fool by stating that "the fear of the Lord is the beginning of knowledge: but fools despise wisdom and instruction." This verse highlights the fundamental difference between the wise and the foolish: the wise person begins with a reverence for God, recognizing that true knowledge and understanding come from Him. In contrast, the fool rejects this foundation, despising the wisdom and instruction that come from God. The fool's disdain for wisdom reflects a deep-seated pride, as he believes that he knows better than the teachings of the Lord. This pride blinds the fool to the truth, leading him to make decisions based on his limited understanding rather than seeking the guidance that could lead him to a better path. In our walk with the Lord, this teaches us the importance of humility and the need to approach life with an open heart and a willingness to learn from God. By rejecting wisdom and instruction, the fool not only separates himself from the knowledge that could lead to a fulfilling and righteous life, but he also distances himself from God, who is the source of all true wisdom.

Proverbs 12:15 further emphasizes the fool's stubbornness and self-deception: "The way of a fool is right in his own eyes: but he that hearkeneth unto counsel is wise." This verse underscores the fool's tendency to trust in his own judgment, even when it is clearly flawed. The fool is convinced of his own rightness, refusing to listen to advice or consider alternative perspectives. This stubbornness is a hallmark of foolishness, as it prevents the fool from growing, learning, and making wiser decisions. In our walk with the Lord, this verse teaches us the importance of being open to counsel, especially when it comes from those who are wise and godly. Listening to others and being willing to consider their insights is a sign of humility and wisdom. The fool's refusal to do so leads him down a path of error, where he is continually making the same mistakes and suffering the consequences of his poor choices. This stubbornness also isolates the fool, as his unwillingness to listen to others creates barriers in relationships and alienates him from those who could offer help and support. In contrast, the wise person seeks counsel, recognizing that others may have valuable insights that can help them navigate life's challenges more effectively.

Proverbs 14:16 adds another layer to our understanding of the fool by highlighting his reckless confidence: "A wise man feareth, and departeth from evil: but the fool rageth, and is confident." This verse contrasts the cautious, prudent behavior of the wise man with the reckless, overconfident behavior of the fool. The wise man recognizes the dangers of evil and takes steps to avoid it, understanding that fear of the Lord and a healthy respect for the consequences of sin are vital to living a righteous life. In contrast, the fool plunges ahead with a false sense of security, driven by his own arrogance and ignorance. This reckless confidence is dangerous, as it leads the fool into situations that he is ill-equipped to handle, exposing him to unnecessary risks and harm. In our walk with the Lord, this verse teaches us the importance of being mindful of the choices we make and the paths we follow. It reminds us that confidence, when not grounded in wisdom and the fear of the Lord, can lead to destruction. The fool's overconfidence is not a sign of strength but of foolishness, as it blinds him to the reality of his situation and the dangers that lie ahead. This reckless behavior often results in the fool's downfall, as he is unable to see the consequences of his actions until it is too late.

The life of the foolish man, as described in these proverbs, is a cautionary tale that warns us of the dangers of pride, stubbornness, and a lack of reverence for God. The fool's rejection of wisdom and instruction, his trust in his own flawed judgment, and his reckless confidence are all traits that lead to a life of turmoil, failure, and ultimately, separation from God. The fool's life is marked by a series of poor decisions, conflicts, and missed opportunities, all stemming from his refusal to humble himself and seek the guidance that could lead him to a better path. In contrast, the wise person, who fears the Lord, seeks counsel, and walks in humility, is able to navigate life's challenges with grace and wisdom, finding success and peace in their relationship with God.

One of the key lessons we can learn from the foolish man is the importance of humility in our walk with the Lord. The fool's pride is his downfall, as it prevents him from recognizing his need for God's wisdom and guidance. In our own lives, we must strive to cultivate a spirit of humility, recognizing that we do not have all the answers and that we need God's help to navigate the complexities of life. This humility opens us up to receiving the wisdom and instruction that God provides, whether through His Word, the counsel of others, or the prompting of the Holy Spirit. By acknowledging our limitations and seeking God's guidance, we can avoid the pitfalls that the fool falls into and live a life that is aligned with God's will.

Another important lesson from the foolish man is the value of seeking wisdom and instruction. The fool's rejection of these is what leads him astray, but for those who desire to walk with the Lord, wisdom is essential. Proverbs teaches us that wisdom begins with the fear of the Lord, which means recognizing God's authority and seeking to live in accordance with His teachings. In our spiritual journey, this means prioritizing time in God's Word, praying for understanding, and being open to the lessons that God wants to teach us through various means. By seeking wisdom, we can grow in our knowledge of God, make better decisions, and live a life that is pleasing to Him. The contrast between the fool and the wise person in Proverbs underscores the importance of this pursuit of wisdom, as it is the foundation for a life that honors God and leads to true fulfillment.

The foolish man also teaches us about the dangers of overconfidence and recklessness. His tendency to "rage" and act with blind confidence in his own abilities often leads to his downfall. This teaches us the importance of being cautious and mindful in our actions, especially when it comes to avoiding sin and temptation. The wise person understands the importance of being vigilant, recognizing the potential dangers of certain choices and taking steps to avoid them. In our walk with the Lord, this means being aware of our weaknesses, seeking accountability, and relying on God's strength to resist temptation. The fool's confidence in his own strength is misplaced, as it leads him into situations that he cannot handle. In contrast, the wise person places their confidence in God, knowing that true strength and security come from Him alone.

In conclusion, the foolish man in Proverbs 1:7, 12:15, and 14:16 provides us with valuable lessons that are essential for our walk with the Lord. His life serves as a warning against the dangers of pride, stubbornness, and reckless confidence, and it highlights the importance of humility, seeking wisdom, and living in reverence to God. By learning from the mistakes of the foolish man, we can strive to be wise in our own spiritual journey, embracing the lessons that God has for us and living a life that is aligned with His will. The fool's life is a reminder that rejecting God's wisdom and relying on our own understanding leads to destruction, while walking in humility, seeking wisdom, and living in the fear of the Lord leads to a life of fulfillment, peace, and closeness with God.

Chapter 3 – The Prudent Man

Proverbs 12:16, "A fool's wrath is presently known: but a prudent man covereth shame," Proverbs 13:16, "Every prudent man dealeth with knowledge: but a fool layeth open his folly," and Proverbs 14:15, "The simple believeth every word: but the prudent man looketh well to his going," offer a clear and insightful picture of the prudent man as described in the book of Proverbs. The prudent man is characterized by his careful consideration, thoughtful decision-making, and ability to exercise self-control. Unlike the foolish man, who is impulsive, easily angered, and quick to make unwise decisions, the prudent man approaches life with caution, wisdom, and a deep understanding of the consequences of his actions. His life is marked by a deliberate and measured approach to challenges, relationships, and opportunities, ensuring that he acts with foresight and discernment. The lessons one can learn from the prudent man in Proverbs are essential for our walk with the Lord, as they teach us the importance of wisdom, self-control, and careful consideration in our daily lives, helping us to live in a way that honors God and leads to a fulfilling and righteous life.

Proverbs 12:16 emphasizes the difference between the prudent man and the fool in terms of how they handle emotions, particularly anger. "A fool's wrath is presently known: but a prudent man covereth shame." This verse highlights the fool's tendency to react impulsively, letting his anger be immediately apparent to everyone around him. The fool lacks self-control and is quick to express his wrath, often leading to regret and further problems. In contrast, the prudent man exercises restraint, choosing to manage his emotions rather than letting them control him. He understands the importance of not allowing his anger to dictate his actions and is careful to avoid bringing shame upon himself or others. The prudent man's ability to cover shame by controlling his temper is a reflection of his wisdom and maturity. In our walk with the Lord, this teaches us the importance of self-control, particularly in how we handle our emotions. By following the example of the prudent man, we can learn to manage our anger and other strong emotions in a way that aligns with God's teachings, avoiding the pitfalls of impulsiveness and ensuring that our actions reflect the love and patience that God calls us to exhibit.

Proverbs 13:16 further illustrates the nature of the prudent man by focusing on his thoughtful and informed approach to decision-making. "Every prudent man dealeth with knowledge: but a fool layeth open his folly." This verse contrasts the prudent man's careful consideration with the fool's reckless behavior. The prudent man does not act hastily or without understanding; instead, he takes the time to gather information, consider the consequences, and make decisions based on knowledge and wisdom. This thoughtful approach allows the prudent man to navigate life's challenges with insight and foresight, avoiding the mistakes that result from ignorance or rashness. In contrast, the fool acts without thinking, making decisions that reveal his lack of understanding and often leading to disastrous results. In our walk with the Lord, this verse teaches us the importance of seeking knowledge and understanding before taking action. It encourages us to be deliberate in our decisions, to seek God's guidance, and to consider the long-term impact of our choices. By emulating the prudent man's approach, we can make decisions that are aligned with God's will and that lead to positive outcomes in our lives and the lives of those around us.

Proverbs 14:15 adds another layer to our understanding of the prudent man by highlighting his cautious and discerning nature. "The simple believeth every word: but the prudent man looketh well to his going." This verse contrasts the simple, or naive, person with the prudent man. The simple person is easily misled, believing whatever they hear without questioning or verifying the information. This gullibility leaves them vulnerable to deception and poor decisions. In contrast, the prudent man is not easily swayed; he takes the time to evaluate the information he receives, considering its source and validity before acting on it. The prudent man's careful consideration of his "going," or the direction of his life, reflects his commitment to making wise and informed decisions. In our walk with the Lord, this verse teaches us the importance of discernment and caution. It reminds us to be critical thinkers, to weigh the advice and information we receive against the truth of God's Word, and to avoid making decisions based on incomplete or misleading information. By adopting the prudent man's approach, we can protect ourselves from being led astray and ensure that our choices are grounded in wisdom and truth.

The life of the prudent man, as described in these proverbs, is a model of thoughtful, informed, and self-controlled living. His approach to life is characterized by a careful consideration of the consequences of his actions, a commitment to seeking knowledge and understanding, and a disciplined management of his emotions. The prudent man's life stands in stark contrast to that of the fool, who acts impulsively, without regard for the consequences, and who is easily led astray by misinformation or emotional impulses. The prudent man's wisdom and discernment are the keys to his success, enabling him to avoid the pitfalls that ensnare the foolish and to build a life that is stable, fulfilling, and aligned with God's will.

One of the key lessons we can learn from the prudent man is the importance of self-control in our walk with the Lord. The prudent man's ability to manage his emotions, particularly anger, is a reflection of his wisdom and maturity. In our own lives, we are often faced with situations that test our patience and self-control, and it is in these moments that we must strive to emulate the prudent man's example. By exercising self-control and not allowing our emotions to dictate our actions, we can avoid the mistakes that come from acting on impulse and instead make choices that reflect God's love, patience, and wisdom. This self-control is a crucial aspect of spiritual maturity, and it is a quality that we must continually cultivate in our relationship with God.

Another important lesson from the prudent man is the value of seeking knowledge and understanding before taking action. The prudent man's careful consideration of his decisions, as described in Proverbs 13:16, is a reminder that we should not rush into decisions without first seeking God's guidance and gaining a full understanding of the situation. In our spiritual journey, this means prioritizing time in prayer, studying God's Word, and seeking counsel from wise and godly individuals. By taking the time to gather information and consider the potential consequences of our actions, we can make decisions that are in line with God's will and that lead to positive outcomes in our lives and the lives of others. This thoughtful approach to decision-making is a hallmark of wisdom, and it is a quality that we should strive to develop in our walk with the Lord.

The prudent man also teaches us the importance of discernment and caution in navigating life's challenges. As Proverbs 14:15 suggests, the prudent man is not easily swayed by every piece of information or advice he receives; instead, he takes the time to evaluate and verify the information before acting on it. In our walk with the Lord, this means being discerning about the influences we allow into our lives, whether they come from people, media, or other sources. It is essential to measure everything against the truth of God's Word and to seek His guidance in all things. By practicing discernment, we can protect ourselves from being led astray by false teachings, harmful influences, or deceptive practices. This cautious approach helps us to remain steadfast in our faith and to make decisions that are grounded in wisdom and truth.

In conclusion, the prudent man in Proverbs 12:16, 13:16, and 14:15 provides us with valuable lessons that are essential for our walk with the Lord. His life serves as a model of thoughtful, informed, and self-controlled living, teaching us the importance of exercising self-control, seeking knowledge and understanding, and practicing discernment in our decisions. By following the example of the prudent man, we can navigate life's challenges with wisdom and grace, making choices that honor God and lead to a fulfilling and righteous life. The prudent man's approach to life is one of careful consideration, thoughtful decision-making, and a deep understanding of the consequences of his actions. These qualities are crucial for anyone who desires to walk closely with the Lord, and they are qualities that we should strive to develop in our own spiritual journey. By embracing the lessons of the prudent man, we can grow in wisdom, avoid the pitfalls of impulsiveness and folly, and live a life that reflects the love, patience, and wisdom of God.

Chapter 4 – The Righteous Man

Proverbs 10:11, "The mouth of a righteous man is a well of life: but violence covereth the mouth of the wicked," Proverbs 12:5, "The thoughts of the righteous are right: but the counsels of the wicked are deceit," and Proverbs 12:26, "The righteous is more excellent than his neighbor: but the way of the wicked seduceth them," provide a powerful and uplifting portrayal of the righteous man as described in the book of Proverbs. The righteous man is characterized by his integrity, his wisdom in speech, his just thoughts, and his exemplary conduct. Unlike the wicked, who are deceitful, violent, and lead others astray, the righteous man embodies qualities that are pleasing to God and beneficial to those around him. His life is a testament to the power of living according to God's principles, demonstrating the blessings that come from walking in righteousness. The lessons one can learn from the righteous man in Proverbs are essential for our walk with the Lord, as they guide us in how to live a life that reflects God's love, truth, and justice, leading to a deeper relationship with Him and a positive impact on the world.

Proverbs 10:11 emphasizes the life-giving power of the righteous man's words: "The mouth of a righteous man is a well of life: but violence covereth the mouth of the wicked." This verse highlights the profound impact that the words of a righteous man can have. Just as a well provides water that sustains life, so too do the words of a righteous man nourish, uplift, and bring life to those who hear them. The righteous man speaks with wisdom, kindness, and truth, offering encouragement, guidance, and hope. His words are not empty or harmful, but they flow from a heart that is aligned with God's will, bringing comfort and strength to others. In contrast, the wicked use their words to harm, deceive, and destroy, spreading violence and discord. In our walk with the Lord, this teaches us the importance of using our words wisely and with intention. By following the example of the righteous man, we can use our speech to build others up, to speak truth, and to share the love of God with those around us. This principle is vital for fostering healthy relationships, creating a positive environment, and being a witness of God's grace and goodness in our lives.

Proverbs 12:5 focuses on the thoughts of the righteous man, stating, "The thoughts of the righteous are right: but the counsels of the wicked are deceit." This verse emphasizes the importance of having a mind that is focused on what is just, true, and good. The righteous man's thoughts are aligned with God's standards of righteousness, leading him to make decisions that are fair, just, and beneficial to all. His thoughts are guided by a desire to do what is right in the eyes of God, and this inner commitment to righteousness shapes his actions and his interactions with others. In contrast, the wicked are driven by deceit, and their thoughts are corrupt, leading them to offer advice and counsel that is harmful and misleading. In our walk with the Lord, this verse teaches us the importance of cultivating a mind that is focused on righteousness. We are called to meditate on God's Word, to seek His guidance in all things, and to allow our thoughts to be shaped by His truth. By doing so, we can ensure that our decisions and actions are rooted in justice and integrity, reflecting the righteousness that God desires in His people.

Proverbs 12:26 provides insight into the conduct of the righteous man, stating, "The righteous is more excellent than his neighbor: but the way of the wicked seduceth them." This verse highlights the superior character and influence of the righteous man compared to those around him. The righteousness of the man sets him apart, making him a model of excellence and integrity. His life serves as a beacon of light, guiding others toward what is good, true, and honorable. However, the verse also warns of the seductive nature of wickedness, which can lead even those with good intentions astray. The righteous man, however, remains steadfast in his commitment to God's ways, resisting the temptations and influences that would pull him away from the path of righteousness. In our walk with the Lord, this verse teaches us the importance of living a life that is above reproach, one that serves as an example to others and that resists the pull of sin and temptation. We are called to be leaders in righteousness, guiding others by our example and helping them to see the value and beauty of living according to God's will.

The life of the righteous man, as described in these proverbs, serves as a powerful example of what it means to live a life that is pleasing to God. His words are a source of life and encouragement, his thoughts are aligned with God's truth, and his conduct is exemplary, setting a standard for others to follow. The righteous man is not perfect, but he strives to live in a way that honors God and reflects His love and justice to the world. This commitment to righteousness is not just about external behavior but is rooted in a heart that is devoted to God and His ways. The righteous man understands that true righteousness comes from a relationship with God and that it is by His grace and guidance that we can live a life that is pleasing to Him.

One of the key lessons we can learn from the righteous man is the importance of speaking words that bring life. The righteous man's words are like a well of life, offering nourishment and encouragement to those who hear them. In our own lives, we must be mindful of how we use our words, recognizing their power to build up or tear down. By speaking words of kindness, truth, and encouragement, we can be a source of blessing to others and reflect the love of God in our interactions. This principle is especially important in our relationships, where our words can have a profound impact on those we love and care for. By following the example of the righteous man, we can use our words to create an environment of love, trust, and mutual respect.

Another important lesson from the righteous man is the value of aligning our thoughts with God's truth. The thoughts of the righteous are right because they are guided by God's wisdom and understanding.

In our walk with the Lord, we must strive to cultivate a mind that is focused on what is true, noble, and just, as described in Philippians 4:8. This involves meditating on God's Word, seeking His guidance in all things, and allowing His truth to shape our thoughts and decisions. By doing so, we can ensure that our actions reflect the righteousness that God desires in us, leading to a life that is marked by integrity, justice, and love.

The righteous man also teaches us the importance of living a life of excellence and integrity. His conduct is more excellent than that of his neighbors because he is committed to living according to God's standards. In our own lives, we must strive to live in a way that reflects the righteousness of God, setting an example for others and being a light in a world that often lacks moral direction. This means being honest in our dealings, treating others with kindness and respect, and standing firm in our convictions, even when it is difficult. By living a life of excellence and integrity, we can be a witness to the transformative power of God's righteousness in our lives and inspire others to seek Him as well.

In conclusion, the righteous man in Proverbs 10:11, 12:5, and 12:26 provides us with valuable lessons that are essential for our walk with the Lord. His life serves as a model of integrity, wisdom, and excellence, teaching us the importance of using our words to bring life, aligning our thoughts with God's truth, and living a life that reflects His righteousness. By following the example of the righteous man, we can grow in our relationship with God, live in a way that is pleasing to Him, and have a positive impact on those around us. The righteous man's life is a testament to the power of living according to God's principles, and it reminds us that true righteousness comes from a heart that is devoted to God and His ways. As we strive to live a life of righteousness, we can be confident that God will guide us, strengthen us, and bless us in our journey, leading us to a life that is fulfilling, meaningful, and aligned with His perfect will.

Chapter 5 – The Wicked Man

Proverbs 4:14, "Enter not into the path of the wicked, and go not in the way of evil men," Proverbs 11:5, "The righteousness of the perfect shall direct his way: but the wicked shall fall by his own wickedness," and Proverbs 14:32, "The wicked is driven away in his wickedness: but the righteous hath hope in his death," paint a vivid and sobering picture of the wicked man as depicted in the book of Proverbs. The wicked man is characterized by his embrace of evil, his moral corruption, and the destructive consequences of his actions. Unlike the righteous, who live according to God's principles and find hope and security in their relationship with Him, the wicked man walks a path that leads to ruin, both in this life and beyond. His life is marked by a disregard for what is right, an inclination towards deceit and wrongdoing, and an ultimate downfall that serves as a warning to all who might be tempted to follow in his footsteps. The lessons one can learn from the wicked man in Proverbs are crucial for our walk with the Lord, as they teach us the importance of avoiding the path of wickedness, embracing righteousness, and living in a way that honors God and leads to true and lasting peace.

Proverbs 4:14 offers a direct and urgent warning: "Enter not into the path of the wicked, and go not in the way of evil men." This verse serves as a clear directive to avoid the ways of the wicked entirely. The path of the wicked is one that leads away from God and towards destruction, filled with deceit, harm, and moral decay. To "enter" this path is to make a choice to engage in behaviors and attitudes that are contrary to God's will. The verse implies that the wicked path is enticing, perhaps appearing as an easy or advantageous route, but it ultimately leads to spiritual and sometimes physical ruin. In our walk with the Lord, this teaches us the importance of discernment and the necessity of choosing the right path, even when the wrong one might seem appealing or easier. We must be vigilant, making conscious decisions to reject evil and avoid situations, influences, or behaviors that could lead us astray. By staying off the path of the wicked, we protect ourselves from the snares of sin and align our lives with the righteous path that God has set before us.

Proverbs 11:5 further elaborates on the fate of the wicked by stating, "The righteousness of the perfect shall direct his way: but the wicked shall fall by his own wickedness." This verse contrasts the guiding power of righteousness with the self-destructive nature of wickedness. The righteous, guided by their integrity and commitment to God's ways, find their paths directed towards good and fulfilling outcomes. In contrast, the wicked man's own actions become his downfall. His wickedness, rooted in selfishness, deceit, and a rejection of God's commandments, leads him to make decisions that are ultimately harmful to himself and others. The phrase "fall by his own wickedness" highlights the idea that the consequences of sin are inherent in the sin itself; the wicked man's choices carry within them the seeds of his own destruction. This teaches us that living a life of sin is not only morally wrong but also inherently self-destructive. In our walk with the Lord, we are reminded to follow the path of righteousness, knowing that it leads to life and peace, while the path of wickedness leads to despair and downfall. This understanding should motivate us to seek God's guidance in all we do, to live according to His principles, and to avoid the pitfalls that come from walking in the ways of the wicked.

Proverbs 14:32 provides a stark contrast between the ultimate end of the wicked and the hope of the righteous: "The wicked is driven away in his wickedness: but the righteous hath hope in his death." This verse highlights the tragic end of the wicked man, who is "driven away" by the very wickedness that he embraced throughout his life. The image of being "driven away" suggests a forceful separation from everything good, a final and irreversible consequence of living a life in opposition to God's will. The wicked man's death is not one of peace or hope, but of despair and separation from God's presence. In contrast, the righteous man, even in death, has hope—hope that is grounded in his relationship with God and the promises of eternal life. This verse teaches us the profound importance of living a life that is aligned with God's righteousness, as it not only brings blessings in this life but also secures our hope for the life to come. The wicked man's fate serves as a powerful warning of the consequences of living in sin, while the hope of the righteous offers a promise of eternal peace and joy with God. In our walk with the Lord, this verse reminds us to focus on living a life of righteousness, knowing that it leads to true and lasting hope, both now and in eternity.

The life of the wicked man, as described in these proverbs, serves as a cautionary tale that warns us of the dangers of embracing sin and rejecting God's ways. His path is one of moral decay, self-deception, and ultimate destruction, both in this life and beyond. The wicked man's life is marked by a series of choices that lead him further and further away from God, resulting in a hardened heart, broken relationships, and a legacy of harm and pain. His story is one of wasted potential and missed opportunities, as he chooses to pursue fleeting pleasures and selfish desires over the lasting peace and fulfillment that come from following God. The wicked man's downfall is not a result of external forces but of his own actions and decisions, which are driven by a rejection of God's wisdom and a refusal to live according to His commandments.

One of the key lessons we can learn from the wicked man is the importance of making conscious and deliberate choices to avoid the path of wickedness. The world is full of temptations and influences that can lead us astray, but as followers of Christ, we must be vigilant in guarding our hearts and minds against these dangers. This means being careful about the company we keep, the media we consume, and the decisions we make daily. By staying rooted in God's Word and seeking His guidance in all things, we can avoid the traps that lead to wickedness and instead walk in the light of His truth. The wicked man's life is a reminder that every choice we make has consequences, and that the path we choose to walk on will ultimately determine our destiny.

Another important lesson from the wicked man is the self-destructive nature of sin. Proverbs 11:5 teaches us that the wicked "shall fall by his own wickedness," highlighting the inherent consequences of living a life of sin. Sin might offer temporary pleasure or satisfaction, but it ultimately leads to pain, regret, and destruction. The wicked man's choices not only harm others but also bring about his own downfall. In our walk with the Lord, this reminds us of the importance of living a life of integrity and righteousness, knowing that God's ways are designed to protect us and lead us to true fulfillment. By avoiding sin and striving to live according to God's commandments, we can experience the peace and joy that come from a life lived in harmony with His will.

The fate of the wicked man, as described in Proverbs 14:32, also teaches us about the importance of living with an eternal perspective. The wicked man is "driven away in his wickedness," facing a bleak and hopeless end because he chose to live in opposition to God's ways. In contrast, the righteous man has hope even in death, knowing that his relationship with God secures his place in eternity. This teaches us the importance of living with our eyes fixed on the eternal promises of God, rather than being consumed by the temporary pleasures and distractions of this world. In our walk with the Lord, we are called to live with an awareness of the bigger picture, understanding that our choices have eternal consequences. By choosing to live a life of righteousness, we not only experience God's blessings in this life but also secure our hope for the life to come.

In conclusion, the wicked man in Proverbs 4:14, 11:5, and 14:32 provides us with valuable lessons that are essential for our walk with the Lord. His life serves as a powerful warning of the dangers of embracing sin, rejecting God's ways, and living a life driven by selfish desires.

The wicked man's path leads to moral decay, self-destruction, and ultimately, separation from God's presence. In contrast, the righteous man, who lives according to God's principles, finds guidance, protection, and hope, both in this life and in eternity. By learning from the wicked man's mistakes, we can make conscious choices to avoid the path of wickedness, to live a life of integrity and righteousness, and to focus on the eternal promises of God. The wicked man's story is a reminder that the choices we make have profound consequences, and that living according to God's will is the only path that leads to true and lasting peace. In our walk with the Lord, we must strive to stay on the righteous path, seeking God's guidance, avoiding the temptations of sin, and living with an eternal perspective that keeps us focused on what truly matters. By doing so, we can experience the fullness of God's blessings and secure our hope for the life to come, knowing that our relationship with Him is our greatest treasure and our ultimate source of security and peace.

Chapter 6 – The Simple Man

Proverbs 1:4, "To give subtilty to the simple, to the young man knowledge and discretion," Proverbs 7:7, "And beheld among the simple ones, I discerned among the youths, a young man void of understanding," and Proverbs 9:4, "Whoso is simple, let him turn in hither: as for him that wanteth understanding, she saith to him," paint a detailed and instructive picture of the simple man as described in the book of Proverbs. The simple man, often portrayed as someone who is naive, inexperienced, and lacking in discernment, is not necessarily wicked or evil, but he is vulnerable to making poor decisions due to his lack of wisdom and understanding. His life is marked by a susceptibility to the influences around him, easily swayed by both good and bad counsel, and often led astray by temptations and wrong choices. The simple man's story serves as a warning to us about the dangers of remaining in a state of ignorance and gullibility, and it underscores the importance of seeking wisdom, growing in understanding, and making intentional choices that lead to a life aligned with God's will. The lessons one can learn from the simple man in Proverbs are crucial for our walk with the Lord, as they teach us the importance of pursuing knowledge, developing discernment, and being vigilant in our spiritual journey to avoid the pitfalls of simplicity and naivety.

Proverbs 1:4 highlights the purpose of wisdom and instruction, which is to give "subtilty to the simple, to the young man knowledge and discretion." This verse underscores the idea that the simple man, though lacking in understanding, has the potential to grow in wisdom if he is willing to learn. The term "subtilty" here refers to prudence or cleverness in navigating life's complexities, which is exactly what the simple man needs. By gaining knowledge and discretion, the simple man can develop the ability to make sound decisions and avoid the traps that might otherwise ensnare him. In our walk with the Lord, this teaches us the importance of being proactive in our pursuit of wisdom. We should not remain content with a superficial understanding of life or faith; instead, we should actively seek to deepen our knowledge of God's Word, to grow in spiritual maturity, and to develop the discernment needed to make wise choices. The simple man's vulnerability serves as a reminder that ignorance is not bliss—it is a dangerous state that can lead to poor decisions and spiritual stagnation. By seeking wisdom, we can move beyond simplicity and begin to live a life that is characterized by insight, understanding, and a closer walk with the Lord.

Proverbs 7:7 provides a vivid illustration of the simple man's susceptibility to temptation: "And beheld among the simple ones, I discerned among the youths, a young man void of understanding." This verse depicts the simple man as someone who is easily led astray because he lacks the understanding needed to recognize the dangers that lie ahead. The context of this proverb is a warning against the seductions of a wayward woman, but the broader lesson applies to all forms of temptation. The simple man's lack of understanding makes him an easy target for those who would lead him into sin, whether through peer pressure, false teachings, or the allure of worldly pleasures. In our walk with the Lord, this verse teaches us the importance of being vigilant and aware of the influences around us. We must not be passive or naive in our approach to life; instead, we should actively seek to grow in understanding so that we can recognize and resist the temptations that seek to pull us away from God's path. The simple man's story is a cautionary tale that warns us of the dangers of spiritual immaturity and the importance of cultivating a strong foundation of knowledge and discernment in our faith journey.

Proverbs 9:4 offers an invitation to the simple man: "Whoso is simple, let him turn in hither: as for him that wanteth understanding, she saith to him." This verse portrays wisdom as a gracious host, calling out to the simple man and inviting him to come and learn. The simple man is not condemned for his lack of understanding; rather, he is encouraged to seek out wisdom and to grow in his knowledge and discernment. This invitation highlights the accessibility of wisdom—anyone who is willing to learn can gain it. The key is a willingness to admit one's need for understanding and to seek out the instruction that leads to growth. In our walk with the Lord, this teaches us that no matter where we are in our spiritual journey, we are always welcome to come and learn from God. He invites us to grow in wisdom, to deepen our relationship with Him, and to gain the understanding we need to live a life that is pleasing to Him. The simple man's story reminds us that spiritual growth is a process that requires humility, a teachable spirit, and a commitment to seeking the truth. By accepting the invitation to wisdom, we can move from a place of naivety and vulnerability to a position of strength and insight, equipped to navigate the challenges of life with godly wisdom.

The life of the simple man, as described in these proverbs, serves as both a warning and an encouragement. His simplicity and lack of understanding make him vulnerable to making poor decisions and falling into temptation, but his story also shows that there is hope for those who seek wisdom. The simple man's life is a reminder that spiritual growth and maturity are not automatic—they require effort, intentionality, and a willingness to learn. The simple man's vulnerability highlights the dangers of remaining in a state of spiritual immaturity, where one is easily swayed by the influences of the world and lacks the discernment needed to make wise choices. However, the simple man's story also encourages us to take action, to seek out the wisdom that God freely offers, and to grow in our understanding of His ways.

One of the key lessons we can learn from the simple man is the importance of actively pursuing wisdom and understanding. The simple man's lack of knowledge and discernment is not a permanent condition; it is something that can be overcome through a commitment to learning and growth. In our own lives, we must not be content with a superficial understanding of our faith or the world around us. Instead, we should strive to deepen our knowledge of God's Word, to seek out godly counsel, and to develop the discernment needed to navigate life's challenges. This requires a willingness to be teachable, to admit when we lack understanding, and to seek out the instruction that leads to growth. By pursuing wisdom, we can move beyond the simplicity that makes us vulnerable to poor decisions and begin to live a life that is characterized by insight, discernment, and a closer relationship with God.

Another important lesson from the simple man is the need to be vigilant and discerning in our spiritual journey. The simple man's lack of understanding makes him an easy target for temptation and deception. In our walk with the Lord, we must be aware of the influences around us and be careful not to be led astray by false teachings, peer pressure, or the allure of worldly pleasures. This requires a commitment to staying grounded in God's Word, to seeking His guidance in all things, and to surrounding ourselves with wise and godly influences. By being vigilant and discerning, we can protect ourselves from the dangers that seek to pull us away from God's path and ensure that our decisions are aligned with His will.

The simple man's story also teaches us the importance of humility and a teachable spirit. Proverbs 9:4's invitation to the simple man to "turn in hither" is a reminder that wisdom is available to all who seek it, but it requires a willingness to admit one's need for understanding and to be open to learning. In our walk with the Lord, we must approach our spiritual journey with humility, recognizing that we do not have all the answers and that we are in constant need of God's guidance and instruction. By maintaining a teachable spirit, we can continue to grow in our faith, to deepen our relationship with God, and to develop the wisdom and discernment needed to live a life that honors Him.

In conclusion, the simple man in Proverbs 1:4, 7:7, and 9:4 provides us with valuable lessons that are essential for our walk with the Lord. His life serves as a warning of the dangers of remaining in a state of spiritual immaturity and a reminder of the importance of actively pursuing wisdom, being vigilant and discerning, and maintaining a humble and teachable spirit. The simple man's vulnerability to poor decisions and temptation highlights the need for growth in understanding and discernment, while his story also offers hope that wisdom is available to all who seek it. By following the lessons learned from the simple man, we can move beyond simplicity and begin to live a life that is characterized by wisdom, insight, and a closer relationship with God. The simple man's story is a call to action for each of us to take our spiritual growth seriously, to seek out the wisdom that God freely offers, and to live in a way that is aligned with His will. As we grow in understanding and discernment, we can navigate the challenges of life with confidence, knowing that we are walking in the wisdom and guidance of the Lord.

Chapter 7 – The Scorner

Proverbs 9:7, "He that reproveth a scorner getteth to himself shame: and he that rebuketh a wicked man getteth himself a blot," Proverbs 14:6, "A scorner seeketh wisdom, and findeth it not: but knowledge is easy unto him that understandeth," and Proverbs 19:29, "Judgments are prepared for scorners, and stripes for the back of fools," provide a clear and sobering picture of the scorner as described in the book of Proverbs. The scorner, also known as the mocker or scoffer, is a person who displays contempt and disdain for wisdom, instruction, and correction. Unlike the simple man, who may lack understanding but is open to learning, or the fool, who is stubborn and self-deceived, the scorner actively rejects and ridicules what is good, true, and wise. His life is marked by arrogance, pride, and a refusal to accept correction, which leads to his downfall and the judgment that inevitably follows. The scorner's attitude and behavior serve as a powerful warning to us about the dangers of pride, the importance of humility, and the necessity of being open to correction and instruction. The lessons one can learn from the scorner in Proverbs are crucial for our walk with the Lord, as they teach us the importance of cultivating a humble and teachable spirit, being receptive to wisdom, and avoiding the destructive path of pride and mockery that leads to spiritual ruin.

Proverbs 9:7 offers a stark warning about the futility and danger of trying to correct a scorner: "He that reproveth a scorner getteth to himself shame: and he that rebuketh a wicked man getteth himself a blot." This verse highlights the scorner's resistance to correction and the negative consequences for those who attempt to reprove him. The scorner, filled with pride and arrogance, not only rejects the correction but often responds with ridicule, contempt, or even hostility. Instead of considering the wisdom offered and adjusting his behavior, the scorner dismisses it outright, viewing himself as above reproach. This attitude creates an environment where constructive feedback is not just unwelcome but met with disdain, leading to further entrenchment in folly. For those who try to offer guidance or correction, engaging with a scorner often results in frustration, shame, and a sense of futility, as their efforts are not only unappreciated but actively opposed. In our walk with the Lord, this teaches us the importance of recognizing when a heart is hardened and when our efforts to correct or guide someone might be counterproductive. It also reminds us to check our own hearts for any signs of scornfulness, ensuring that we remain open to correction and instruction, recognizing that true wisdom comes from being teachable and humble. The scorner's example warns us of the dangers of pride, which can close our hearts and minds to the very guidance that could lead us to growth and transformation.

Proverbs 14:6 provides further insight into the scorner's relationship with wisdom: "A scorner seeketh wisdom, and findeth it not: but knowledge is easy unto him that understandeth." This verse illustrates the futility of the scorner's search for wisdom, which is ultimately fruitless because of his attitude. While the scorner may outwardly seek wisdom or claim to desire understanding, his pride and mockery create a barrier that prevents him from truly grasping it. Wisdom requires a heart that is open, humble, and ready to learn, but the scorner's arrogance blinds him to the truths that could lead to genuine knowledge and insight. In contrast, those who are humble and understanding find knowledge with ease because they approach it with the right attitude—one of reverence, curiosity, and a willingness to be taught. In our walk with the Lord, this verse teaches us that the pursuit of wisdom is not just about seeking knowledge but about the posture of our hearts as we seek it. If we approach God's wisdom with a scornful, prideful attitude, we will find that it eludes us, no matter how earnestly we search. However, if we seek wisdom with humility and a genuine desire to grow, we will find that God's truths are revealed to us with clarity and understanding. The scorner's failure to find wisdom serves as a cautionary tale, reminding us that our attitude and approach to learning are just as important as the act of seeking knowledge itself.

Proverbs 19:29 serves as a solemn reminder of the consequences that await the scorner: "Judgments are prepared for scorners, and stripes for the back of fools." This verse underscores the inevitable judgment and discipline that come to those who persist in their scornful ways. The scorner, by rejecting wisdom, instruction, and correction, sets himself on a path that leads to judgment. His prideful refusal to listen or change invites consequences that are both severe and just. The "judgments" mentioned in this verse are not arbitrary but are the natural outcomes of a life lived in opposition to God's ways. The scorner's behavior not only harms himself but also disrupts the community and leads others astray, making the need for judgment and correction all the more necessary. In our walk with the Lord, this verse teaches us that there are serious consequences for rejecting God's wisdom and for living a life marked by pride and mockery. It reminds us of the importance of being humble and open to correction, understanding that God's discipline, though sometimes painful, is ultimately for our good and intended to bring us back to the right path. The scorner's fate is a warning that pride leads to destruction, while humility and a willingness to be corrected lead to life and growth.

The life of the scorner, as described in these proverbs, serves as a powerful example of the dangers of pride, arrogance, and a closed heart. His story is one of wasted potential, missed opportunities, and a hardening of the heart that leads to inevitable judgment. The scorner's refusal to accept correction, his mockery of wisdom, and his disdain for instruction create a life that is increasingly isolated, resistant to change, and ultimately self-destructive. His journey is not just a cautionary tale for others but a reflection of the potential consequences that await anyone who allows pride to take root in their heart. The scorner's life is marked by a refusal to grow, to learn, or to change, leading him further away from the wisdom that could bring healing, growth, and transformation. His story reminds us that pride is one of the most significant barriers to spiritual growth and that humility is the key to unlocking the wisdom and understanding that God desires to impart to us.

One of the key lessons we can learn from the scorner is the importance of cultivating a humble and teachable spirit. The scorner's downfall is rooted in his prideful refusal to listen to others, to accept correction, and to acknowledge his need for growth. In our own lives, we must guard against the temptation to believe that we know it all or that we are beyond the need for instruction. Instead, we should approach our walk with the Lord with humility, recognizing that we are all works in progress and that there is always more to learn. By being open to correction and willing to receive instruction, we can avoid the pitfalls of pride and grow in wisdom, knowledge, and understanding. This requires a daily commitment to self-reflection, prayer, and a willingness to listen to the voices of those who offer godly counsel, even when it challenges us or makes us uncomfortable.

Another important lesson from the scorner is the need to be receptive to wisdom and to approach the pursuit of knowledge with the right attitude. The scorner's failure to find wisdom, despite seeking it, highlights the importance of our approach to learning. If we seek wisdom with a prideful or scornful heart, we will find that it remains out of reach, no matter how diligently we search. In contrast, when we seek wisdom with humility, reverence, and a genuine desire to grow, we find that God's truths are readily available to us. In our walk with the Lord, this means approaching our study of Scripture, our time in prayer, and our engagement with spiritual disciplines with an open and humble heart, ready to receive what God wants to teach us. By doing so, we position ourselves to gain the wisdom that leads to life, growth, and a deeper relationship with God.

The scorner's story also teaches us about the consequences of rejecting God's wisdom and instruction. Proverbs 19:29's reminder that "judgments are prepared for scorners" serves as a warning that there are serious consequences for living a life marked by pride, mockery, and a refusal to accept correction. In our walk with the Lord, we must remember that God's discipline, though sometimes painful, is ultimately for our good. It is intended to bring us back to the right path, to correct our course, and to help us grow in righteousness. The scorner's fate is a reminder that pride leads to destruction, while humility leads to life. By embracing God's discipline and being willing to change, we can avoid the judgment that comes from a hardened heart and instead experience the blessings of a life lived in alignment with God's will.

In conclusion, the scorner in Proverbs 9:7, 14:6, and 19:29 provides us with valuable lessons that are essential for our walk with the Lord. His life serves as a powerful warning of the dangers of pride, arrogance, and a refusal to accept correction. The scorner's attitude and behavior lead to a life of isolation, missed opportunities, and ultimately, judgment. However, his story also offers us important insights into the importance of cultivating a humble and teachable spirit, being receptive to wisdom, and embracing God's discipline as a means of growth and transformation. By learning from the scorner's mistakes, we can guard against the pitfalls of pride and ensure that we remain

open to the wisdom and instruction that God wants to impart to us. The scorner's life is a reminder that humility is the key to unlocking the blessings of wisdom, understanding, and a deeper relationship with God. In our walk with the Lord, we must strive to approach our spiritual journey with an attitude of humility, a willingness to learn, and a readiness to receive correction. By doing so, we can avoid the destructive path of the scorner and instead experience the fullness of life that comes from walking in the wisdom and grace of God.

Chapter 8 – The Lazy Man/Sluggard

Proverbs 6:6, "Go to the ant, thou sluggard; consider her ways, and be wise," Proverbs 10:26, "As vinegar to the teeth, and as smoke to the eyes, so is the sluggard to them that send him," and Proverbs 13:4, "The soul of the sluggard desireth, and hath nothing: but the soul of the diligent shall be made fat," provide a vivid and instructive depiction of the lazy man, also known as the sluggard, as described in the book of Proverbs. The lazy man is characterized by his reluctance to work, his lack of initiative, and the numerous negative consequences that result from his idleness and procrastination. Unlike the diligent man, who is proactive, responsible, and reaps the rewards of his efforts, the sluggard shirks his responsibilities, avoids hard work, and ultimately suffers the consequences of his laziness. His life is marked by unfulfilled desires, missed opportunities, and a general state of dissatisfaction and unproductiveness. The lazy man's story serves as a powerful warning about the dangers of slothfulness and the importance of diligence, responsibility, and hard work in every aspect of life, including our walk with the Lord. The lessons one can learn from the lazy man in Proverbs are crucial for our spiritual journey, as they teach us the value of discipline, the necessity of active engagement in our faith, and the importance of using our time and talents wisely to fulfill God's purpose for our lives.

Proverbs 6:6 uses the example of the ant to teach the lazy man a valuable lesson: "Go to the ant, thou sluggard; consider her ways, and be wise." The ant, though small and seemingly insignificant, is a model of industriousness and foresight. It works diligently to gather food and prepare for the future, without needing supervision or prompting. The ant's behavior contrasts sharply with that of the sluggard, who avoids work and fails to plan ahead. This verse encourages the lazy man to observe the ant and learn the value of hard work, self-motivation, and preparation. In our walk with the Lord, this teaches us the importance of being proactive in our faith. Just as the ant diligently gathers food, we must be diligent in seeking spiritual nourishment through prayer, reading the Bible, and participating in fellowship with other believers. The sluggard's tendency to procrastinate and avoid effort can be spiritually dangerous, leading to a weak and unproductive faith life. By following the example of the ant, we can develop the discipline and diligence needed to grow in our relationship with God and to be effective in our service to Him.

Proverbs 10:26 highlights the negative impact that the sluggard has on others: "As vinegar to the teeth, and as smoke to the eyes, so is the sluggard to them that send him." This verse compares the sluggard to vinegar and smoke, both of which are irritating and unpleasant. Just as vinegar causes discomfort to the teeth and smoke irritates the eyes, the sluggard causes frustration and disappointment to those who rely on him. His laziness leads to unreliability and failure to fulfill responsibilities, making him a burden rather than a help. In our walk with the Lord, this teaches us the importance of being dependable and responsible in our commitments, whether in our personal lives, our work, or our service to others. Laziness not only hinders our own progress but also affects those around us, leading to strained relationships and lost trust. By being diligent and responsible, we can build strong, reliable relationships and be a positive influence on those around us. The sluggard's example serves as a warning that our actions, or lack thereof, have consequences not only for ourselves but also for those who depend on us. In our spiritual life, this means being faithful in our commitments to God and others, understanding that our diligence reflects our love for God and our desire to serve Him faithfully.

Proverbs 13:4 contrasts the desires of the sluggard with those of the diligent: "The soul of the sluggard desireth, and hath nothing: but the soul of the diligent shall be made fat." This verse highlights the futility of the sluggard's desires. While he may long for success, comfort, or fulfillment, his unwillingness to put in the necessary effort leaves him empty-handed. In contrast, the diligent person, who works hard and perseveres, is rewarded with abundance and satisfaction. The sluggard's laziness leads to unfulfilled dreams and a life of frustration, while the diligent person experiences the fruits of their labor. In our walk with the Lord, this teaches us the importance of being diligent in pursuing our spiritual goals. Just as the sluggard's desires remain unfulfilled due to his inaction, so too will our spiritual growth be stunted if we are lazy in our pursuit of God. Diligence in prayer, study, and obedience to God's Word leads to spiritual richness and a deep, fulfilling relationship with Him. The sluggard's story is a reminder that mere desire is not enough; it must be accompanied by action and perseverance. In our spiritual journey, this means actively seeking God, consistently engaging in spiritual disciplines, and persevering in our faith, even when it is challenging. By doing so, we can experience the fullness of life that God promises to those who diligently seek Him.

The life of the lazy man, as described in these proverbs, serves as a powerful example of the consequences of slothfulness and the importance of diligence in all areas of life. The sluggard's reluctance to work, his failure to fulfill responsibilities, and his unfulfilled desires all lead to a life of dissatisfaction and missed opportunities. His story is not just a warning about the dangers of physical laziness but also about the spiritual dangers of being idle and unproductive in our walk with the Lord. The sluggard's life is marked by a lack of purpose, direction, and fulfillment, which are the natural results of avoiding hard work and discipline. In contrast, the diligent person, who embraces responsibility and works hard, experiences the rewards of their efforts, both in this life and in their relationship with God.

One of the key lessons we can learn from the lazy man is the importance of discipline and hard work in our spiritual life. Just as the sluggard's laziness leads to unproductiveness and frustration, so too does spiritual laziness lead to a stagnant and unfulfilling faith.

In our walk with the Lord, we must be disciplined in our spiritual practices, such as prayer, reading the Bible, and serving others. These disciplines require effort and commitment, but they are essential for spiritual growth and a deep relationship with God. The sluggard's example serves as a reminder that spiritual growth does not happen by accident; it requires intentionality, perseverance, and a willingness to put in the necessary effort. By being diligent in our spiritual practices, we can experience the richness of a life lived in close communion with God.

Another important lesson from the lazy man is the need to be reliable and responsible in our commitments. The sluggard's unreliability causes frustration and disappointment to those who depend on him, highlighting the importance of being dependable in our relationships and responsibilities. In our walk with the Lord, this means being faithful in our commitments to God, to our families, and to our communities. Laziness and unreliability not only hinder our own progress but also damage our relationships and our witness to others. By being diligent and responsible, we can build strong, trustworthy relationships and be a positive influence on those around us. The sluggard's story is a reminder that our actions have consequences, and that our diligence and reliability are reflections of our love for God and our desire to serve Him faithfully.

The sluggard's unfulfilled desires, as described in Proverbs 13:4, also teach us about the importance of perseverance and action in achieving our goals. The sluggard's desires remain unfulfilled because he is unwilling to put in the necessary effort to achieve them. In contrast, the diligent person, who works hard and perseveres, experiences the satisfaction and abundance that come from their efforts. In our walk with the Lord, this teaches us that mere desire is not enough; it must be accompanied by action and perseverance. Whether it is growing in our faith, overcoming challenges, or fulfilling our God-given purpose, we must be willing to put in the effort and persevere through difficulties.

The sluggard's story is a reminder that spiritual growth and fulfillment require more than just good intentions; they require commitment, effort, and perseverance. By being diligent in our pursuit of God and His purposes for our lives, we can experience the fullness of life that He promises to those who seek Him with all their hearts.

In conclusion, the lazy man, or sluggard, in Proverbs 6:6, 10:26, and 13:4 provides us with valuable lessons that are essential for our walk with the Lord. His life serves as a powerful warning of the dangers of slothfulness, unreliability, and unfulfilled desires. The sluggard's reluctance to work, his failure to fulfill responsibilities, and his unproductive life highlight the importance of discipline, responsibility, and hard work in our spiritual journey. In contrast, the diligent person, who embraces responsibility and works hard, experiences the rewards of their efforts, both in this life and in their relationship with God. By learning from the lazy man's mistakes, we can avoid the pitfalls of slothfulness and embrace the discipline and diligence needed to grow in our relationship with God, to fulfill our responsibilities, and to live a life of purpose and fulfillment. The lazy man's story is a reminder that spiritual growth requires intentionality, effort, and perseverance, and that our diligence and reliability are reflections of our love for God and our desire to serve Him faithfully. In our walk with the Lord, we must strive to be diligent, disciplined, and responsible, understanding that these qualities are essential for a deep, fulfilling relationship with God and a life that honors Him. By doing so, we can experience the richness and abundance of a life lived in close communion with God, fulfilling His purposes for our lives and being a positive influence on those around us.

Chapter 9 – The Diligent Man

Proverbs 10:4, "He becometh poor that dealeth with a slack hand: but the hand of the diligent maketh rich," Proverbs 12:24, "The hand of the diligent shall bear rule: but the slothful shall be under tribute," and Proverbs 22:29, "Seest thou a man diligent in his business? he shall stand before kings; he shall not stand before mean men," present a compelling and uplifting portrait of the diligent man as described in the book of Proverbs. The diligent man is characterized by his hard work, perseverance, and a consistent commitment to excellence in all that he undertakes. Unlike the lazy man or the sluggard, who avoids responsibility and suffers the consequences of idleness, the diligent man embraces his duties with vigor and determination, leading to success, honor, and fulfillment. His life is marked by a steady progression towards his goals, a reputation for reliability and integrity, and the rewards that come from his dedication. The diligent man's story serves as an inspiring example of the virtues of hard work, perseverance, and faithfulness, offering valuable lessons for anyone seeking to live a life that honors God and fulfills His purpose. The lessons one can learn from the diligent man in Proverbs are crucial for our walk with the Lord, as they teach us the importance of diligence in our spiritual journey, the value of working with excellence in all that we do, and the rewards that come from faithfully serving God with all our hearts.

Proverbs 10:4 emphasizes the direct connection between diligence and prosperity: "He becometh poor that dealeth with a slack hand: but the hand of the diligent maketh rich." This verse highlights the consequences of laziness and the benefits of hard work. The "slack hand" represents a lazy, careless approach to work that inevitably leads to poverty and lack. In contrast, the "hand of the diligent" signifies a person who works hard, pays attention to detail, and remains committed to their tasks until they are completed. This diligent approach leads to wealth, not just in a financial sense, but in the broader sense of a life rich with purpose, satisfaction, and fulfillment. The diligent man does not shy away from hard work; he understands that success requires effort and perseverance, and he is willing to invest the time and energy needed to achieve his goals. In our walk with the Lord, this teaches us the importance of being diligent in our spiritual practices. Just as the diligent man works hard to achieve success in his endeavors, we must be diligent in our pursuit of God, committing ourselves to regular prayer, study of the Scriptures, and active participation in the life of the church. Diligence in our spiritual life leads to a deeper relationship with God, greater spiritual maturity, and the fulfillment of God's purpose for our lives. The diligent man's example encourages us to take our spiritual growth seriously, to invest the necessary time and effort, and to remain committed to our faith, knowing that our diligence will be rewarded by God.

Proverbs 12:24 highlights the leadership and influence that come from diligence: "The hand of the diligent shall bear rule: but the slothful shall be under tribute." This verse contrasts the positions of the diligent and the lazy, showing that diligence leads to positions of authority and influence, while laziness results in subjugation and a lack of control over one's life. The diligent man, through his hard work and reliability, earns the respect and trust of others, which often leads to opportunities for leadership and greater responsibility. His diligence not only benefits him personally but also positions him to positively impact others and contribute to the greater good. In contrast, the slothful person, who avoids work and responsibility, finds himself at the mercy of others, with little control over his circumstances. In our walk with the Lord, this verse teaches us that diligence in our spiritual life can lead to spiritual leadership and influence. When we are diligent in our faith, others take notice, and we may be called upon to lead, mentor, or guide others in their spiritual journey. Diligence in our relationship with God equips us to serve Him more effectively and to be a positive influence in the lives of others. The diligent man's example challenges us to take our responsibilities seriously, to work hard in all that we do, and to be faithful in the tasks that God has entrusted to us. By doing so, we can be used by God in significant ways, making a lasting impact on those around us and advancing His kingdom.

Proverbs 22:29 underscores the recognition and honor that come from diligence: "Seest thou a man diligent in his business? he shall stand before kings; he shall not stand before mean men." This verse illustrates the high regard and respect that diligent people earn as a result of their hard work and excellence. The diligent man is not only successful in his endeavors, but he also gains the attention and admiration of those in positions of power and influence. His dedication to his work and his commitment to doing it well lead to opportunities for advancement and recognition, allowing him to "stand before kings" and be honored for his efforts. In our walk with the Lord, this verse teaches us that diligence in our spiritual and worldly responsibilities can lead to God's favor and opportunities for greater influence. When we are diligent in our work, whether it is in our careers, our ministries, or our personal lives, we bring glory to God and open doors for greater service and impact. The diligent man's example inspires us to strive for excellence in all that we do, understanding that our work is a reflection of our faith and our commitment to God. By being diligent in our work, we not only achieve success but also have the opportunity to influence others and bring glory to God through our efforts.

The life of the diligent man, as described in these proverbs, serves as a powerful example of the rewards and benefits of hard work, perseverance, and faithfulness. His life is marked by success, influence, and honor, all of which are the direct results of his commitment to diligence. The diligent man understands that success does not come easily or automatically; it requires consistent effort, a strong work ethic, and a commitment to doing one's best in every task. His story is not just about achieving personal success but also about the broader impact that diligence can have on others and on the world. The diligent man's life is a testament to the fact that hard work and perseverance are not just practical virtues but also spiritual ones, as they reflect a deep commitment to God's purpose and a desire to serve Him faithfully in all areas of life.

One of the key lessons we can learn from the diligent man is the importance of perseverance in our spiritual journey. Just as the diligent man does not give up when faced with challenges or obstacles, we must also persevere in our faith, even when it is difficult or when the results are not immediately visible. In our walk with the Lord, perseverance is essential for spiritual growth and maturity. It is through consistent, diligent effort that we grow in our relationship with God, overcome spiritual challenges, and become more like Christ. The diligent man's example encourages us to remain steadfast in our spiritual practices, to continue seeking God's presence, and to trust that our efforts will bear fruit in due time.

Another important lesson from the diligent man is the value of excellence in all that we do. The diligent man's commitment to doing his work well leads to success, recognition, and opportunities for greater influence. In our walk with the Lord, this teaches us that our work, whatever it may be, should be done with excellence, as a reflection of our love for God and our desire to honor Him. Whether we are working in our careers, serving in our communities, or fulfilling our responsibilities at home, we should strive to do our best, knowing that our work is a form of worship and service to God. The diligent man's example challenges us to approach every task with a spirit of excellence, understanding that our efforts have a greater purpose and that they can bring glory to God.

The diligent man's story also teaches us about the rewards of faithfulness. Proverbs 12:24's reminder that "the hand of the diligent shall bear rule" highlights the connection between diligence and leadership. When we are faithful in our responsibilities and committed to doing our best, we gain the trust and respect of others, which often leads to opportunities for greater influence and leadership. In our walk with the Lord, this teaches us that faithfulness in small things leads to greater responsibilities and opportunities to serve. When we are diligent in our spiritual life, in our work, and in our relationships, God entrusts us with more significant roles and opportunities to make an impact. The diligent man's example encourages us to be faithful in the tasks that God has given us, knowing that our diligence will be rewarded with opportunities to serve Him in even greater ways.

In conclusion, the diligent man in Proverbs 10:4, 12:24, and 22:29 provides us with valuable lessons that are essential for our walk with the Lord. His life serves as an inspiring example of the virtues of hard work, perseverance, and faithfulness. The diligent man's commitment to excellence, his perseverance in the face of challenges, and his faithfulness in his responsibilities lead to success, recognition, and opportunities for greater influence. In contrast to the lazy man, who suffers the consequences of idleness and lack of effort, the diligent man reaps the rewards of his hard work and dedication. By learning from the diligent man's example, we can embrace the discipline and perseverance needed to grow in our relationship with God, to fulfill our responsibilities with excellence, and to live a life that honors Him. The diligent man's story is a reminder that success and fulfillment come from consistent, diligent effort and that our work, when done with excellence and faithfulness, can have a lasting impact on others and bring glory to God. In our walk with the Lord, we must strive to be diligent in all that we do, understanding that our efforts are not just for our benefit but

are also a reflection of our commitment to God's purpose and our desire to serve Him faithfully. By doing so, we can experience the fullness of life that God promises to those who diligently seek Him and who work hard to fulfill His purpose for their lives.

Chapter 10 – The Understanding Man

Proverbs 10:23, "It is as sport to a fool to do mischief: but a man of understanding hath wisdom," Proverbs 14:29, "He that is slow to wrath is of great understanding: but he that is hasty of spirit exalteth folly," and Proverbs 15:21, "Folly is joy to him that is destitute of wisdom: but a man of understanding walketh uprightly," collectively paint a picture of the understanding man as described in the book of Proverbs. The understanding man is characterized by his deep discernment, patience, and commitment to living a life of wisdom and righteousness. Unlike the fool, who finds joy in mischief and folly, the man of understanding values wisdom and approaches life with a thoughtful and discerning spirit. His actions are guided by a deep awareness of God's principles and a careful consideration of the consequences of his choices. The understanding man's life serves as a powerful example of the virtues of patience, discernment, and wisdom, offering valuable lessons for anyone seeking to walk faithfully with the Lord. The lessons one can learn from the understanding man in Proverbs are essential for our spiritual journey, as they teach us the importance of cultivating wisdom, exercising self-control, and living in a way that reflects God's righteousness and love.

Proverbs 10:23 contrasts the behavior of the fool with that of the understanding man: "It is as sport to a fool to do mischief: but a man of understanding hath wisdom." This verse highlights the stark difference between the fool, who takes pleasure in doing wrong, and the man of understanding, who treasures wisdom. For the fool, mischief and wrongdoing are sources of amusement; he lacks the moral compass that guides his actions towards what is good and right. In contrast, the understanding man is not only aware of the difference between right and wrong, but he actively chooses the path of wisdom. His understanding leads him to value wisdom above all, knowing that it is the key to living a life that honors God and benefits others. In our walk with the Lord, this teaches us the importance of prioritizing wisdom in our decisions and actions. The understanding man's example encourages us to seek God's wisdom in all things, to avoid the folly of wrongdoing, and to live in a way that reflects God's love and truth. By valuing wisdom as the understanding man does, we can make choices that lead to a life of integrity, purpose, and fulfillment, rather than one marked by the fleeting pleasures of folly.

Proverbs 14:29 further explores the character of the understanding man by emphasizing his patience and self-control: "He that is slow to wrath is of great understanding: but he that is hasty of spirit exalteth folly." This verse highlights the connection between understanding and the ability to control one's temper. The understanding man is slow to anger because he recognizes the destructive power of uncontrolled wrath and the importance of maintaining a calm and thoughtful demeanor. His patience is not a sign of weakness but of strength, as it reflects his deep understanding of the consequences of hasty and emotional reactions. In contrast, those who are quick to anger act foolishly, often making decisions they later regret and causing harm to themselves and others. In our walk with the Lord, this teaches us the value of patience and self-control. The understanding man's ability to remain calm and measured in difficult situations is a model for how we should approach challenges and conflicts in our own lives. By being slow to anger and quick to listen, we can avoid the pitfalls of rash decisions and ensure that our actions are guided by wisdom and love. This principle is especially important in our relationships, where patience and understanding are key to resolving conflicts and building strong, healthy connections with others.

Proverbs 15:21 offers another insight into the nature of the understanding man: "Folly is joy to him that is destitute of wisdom: but a man of understanding walketh uprightly." This verse contrasts the behavior of those who lack wisdom with that of the understanding man. For those who are "destitute of wisdom," foolish behavior brings joy because they lack the discernment to see the consequences of their actions. They are short-sighted, focused on immediate gratification rather than long-term well-being. In contrast, the understanding man "walketh uprightly," meaning he lives with integrity and a commitment to doing what is right. His understanding allows him to see beyond the momentary pleasures of folly and to choose a path that is aligned with God's righteousness. In our walk with the Lord, this teaches us the importance of living with integrity and making choices that reflect our commitment to God's principles. The understanding man's example challenges us to consider the long-term impact of our actions, to prioritize righteousness over immediate gratification, and to walk in a way that honors God. By doing so, we can avoid the pitfalls of folly and experience the blessings that come from living a life of integrity and wisdom.

The life of the understanding man, as described in these proverbs, serves as a powerful example of the importance of wisdom, patience, and integrity in our spiritual journey. His deep discernment and commitment to wisdom set him apart from those who are foolish and short-sighted. The understanding man's life is marked by a thoughtful approach to challenges, a controlled and patient response to conflicts, and a consistent commitment to living in accordance with God's principles. His story is not just a contrast to the behavior of the fool but a model for how we should strive to live as followers of Christ. The understanding man's example teaches us that true wisdom is not just about knowing what is right but about applying that knowledge in our daily lives, in our decisions, and in our interactions with others.

One of the key lessons we can learn from the understanding man is the importance of cultivating wisdom in our spiritual life. Just as the understanding man values wisdom and seeks to apply it in all areas of his life, we too must prioritize the pursuit of wisdom in our walk with the Lord. This means regularly studying God's Word, seeking His guidance in prayer, and being open to the counsel of others. Wisdom is not something we acquire overnight; it is the result of a continuous and intentional effort to grow in our understanding of God and His ways. The understanding man's example encourages us to make this pursuit of wisdom a central focus in our lives, knowing that it will guide us in making decisions that honor God and lead to a life of purpose and fulfillment.

Another important lesson from the understanding man is the value of patience and self-control. Proverbs 14:29's emphasis on being "slow to wrath" reminds us that patience is a critical aspect of understanding. The understanding man's ability to remain calm and measured in difficult situations reflects his deep trust in God and his commitment to living in a way that reflects God's love and grace. In our walk with the Lord, we must strive to develop this same patience and self-control, particularly when we face challenges or conflicts. By being slow to anger and quick to listen, we can respond to situations with wisdom and grace, avoiding the destructive consequences of rash decisions and emotional outbursts. The understanding man's example challenges us to approach every situation with a calm and thoughtful demeanor, trusting that God will guide us in responding in a way that honors Him.

The understanding man's commitment to walking uprightly, as described in Proverbs 15:21, also teaches us about the importance of integrity in our spiritual journey. His understanding allows him to see beyond the immediate pleasures of folly and to choose a path that is aligned with God's righteousness. In our walk with the Lord, we must strive to live with the same integrity, making choices that reflect our commitment to God's principles and our desire to honor Him in all that we do. This means being honest, trustworthy, and faithful in our relationships, our work, and our service to others. The understanding man's example challenges us to consider the long-term impact of our actions and to prioritize righteousness over immediate gratification. By walking uprightly, we can avoid the pitfalls of folly and experience the blessings that come from living a life of integrity and wisdom.

In conclusion, the understanding man in Proverbs 10:23, 14:29, and 15:21 provides us with valuable lessons that are essential for our walk with the Lord. His life serves as a powerful example of the virtues of wisdom, patience, and integrity. The understanding man's deep discernment, his controlled and patient response to challenges, and his commitment to living in accordance with God's principles set him apart from those who are foolish and short-sighted. By learning from the understanding man's example, we can cultivate the wisdom needed to make decisions that honor God, develop the patience and self-control necessary to navigate life's challenges with grace, and live with integrity in all areas of our lives. The understanding man's story is a reminder that true wisdom is not just about knowing what is right but about applying that knowledge in our daily lives, in our decisions, and in our interactions with others. In our walk with the Lord, we must strive to be understanding, wise, and patient, knowing that these qualities will guide us in living a life that reflects God's love and truth. By doing so, we can experience the fullness of life that God promises to those who seek Him with all their hearts and who live in accordance with His wisdom and righteousness.

Chapter 11 – The Angry Man

Proverbs 14:17, "He that is soon angry dealeth foolishly: and a man of wicked devices is hated," Proverbs 22:24, "Make no friendship with an angry man; and with a furious man thou shalt not go," and Proverbs 29:22, "An angry man stirreth up strife, and a furious man aboundeth in transgression," provide a vivid and cautionary portrayal of the angry man as described in the book of Proverbs. The angry man is characterized by his quick temper, his tendency to act irrationally, and the destructive impact his anger has on himself and those around him. Unlike the patient and understanding man, who exercises self-control and wisdom, the angry man is often impulsive, allowing his emotions to govern his actions, which leads to conflict, division, and a host of other negative consequences. His life is marked by turmoil, strained relationships, and an inability to maintain peace and harmony, both within himself and in his interactions with others. The lessons one can learn from the angry man in Proverbs are crucial for our walk with the Lord, as they teach us the importance of cultivating self-control, practicing patience, and seeking peace in our relationships and daily lives.

Proverbs 14:17 warns of the foolishness that comes with a quick temper: "He that is soon angry dealeth foolishly: and a man of wicked devices is hated." This verse highlights the dangers of allowing anger to control one's actions. A person who is quick to anger is prone to making rash decisions without considering the consequences, often leading to foolish and regrettable outcomes. The verse also connects anger with foolishness, suggesting that when anger is not kept in check, it clouds judgment and leads to actions that are not only unwise but also harmful. The angry man, in his haste to act out of anger, often overlooks the broader impact of his behavior, damaging relationships, and creating unnecessary conflicts. In our walk with the Lord, this teaches us the importance of exercising self-control and being mindful of our emotions. By recognizing the dangers of quick anger, we can take steps to pause, reflect, and seek God's guidance before reacting. The angry man's example serves as a reminder that impulsive actions driven by anger can have long-lasting negative effects, and that wisdom requires us to slow down, consider the consequences, and respond with calmness and understanding. In practicing self-control, we align ourselves with God's will, which calls us to be peacemakers and to reflect His love and patience in our interactions with others.

Proverbs 22:24 offers a strong admonition against forming close relationships with those who are prone to anger: "Make no friendship with an angry man; and with a furious man thou shalt not go." This verse underscores the influence that an angry person can have on those around him, warning that associating with someone who is quick to anger can lead to negative outcomes. The angry man's volatile nature not only affects his own life but also has the potential to drag others into unnecessary conflicts and strife. By aligning oneself with someone who is frequently angry, there is a risk of being drawn into their patterns of behavior, which can include arguments, disputes, and even physical confrontations. In our walk with the Lord, this teaches us the importance of choosing our relationships wisely and surrounding ourselves with people who reflect the qualities of patience, peace, and wisdom. While it is important to love and minister to everyone, including those who struggle with anger, we must also be cautious about forming close ties with individuals whose anger can negatively influence our own behavior and spiritual growth. The angry man's example reminds us that the company we keep has a significant impact on our lives, and that we should seek to build relationships that encourage us to grow in godliness, rather than pull us into destructive patterns.

Proverbs 29:22 further explores the consequences of anger, stating, "An angry man stirreth up strife, and a furious man aboundeth in transgression." This verse highlights the ripple effect of an angry disposition, showing that an angry person often becomes a source of conflict and division. The angry man's inability to control his temper leads to strife not only in his own life but also in the lives of those around him. His anger becomes a catalyst for arguments, misunderstandings, and broken relationships, creating an environment of tension and discord. Furthermore, the verse indicates that anger often leads to other sins, as a "furious man aboundeth in transgression." When anger is left unchecked, it can drive a person to act out in ways that are contrary to God's will, leading to a cycle of sin that further distances the individual from God and from others. In our walk with the Lord, this teaches us the importance of striving for peace and being mindful of the impact our emotions have on our actions. The angry man's tendency to stir up strife serves as a warning that unresolved anger can lead to a host of other sins and problems, all of which hinder our relationship with God and with those around us. By seeking to resolve our anger in healthy and constructive ways, we can prevent it from escalating into more serious issues and can work towards building relationships that are characterized by understanding, forgiveness, and love.

The life of the angry man, as described in these proverbs, serves as a powerful example of the destructive power of uncontrolled anger and the importance of cultivating a spirit of patience and self-control. His quick temper, impulsive actions, and tendency to stir up conflict all lead to a life marked by turmoil and division. The angry man's story is not just a warning about the dangers of anger but also a call to pursue the qualities that lead to peace, harmony, and spiritual growth. The angry man's life is a reminder that while anger is a natural human emotion, it must be managed carefully and channeled in ways that align with God's will. Left unchecked, anger can lead to foolish decisions, broken relationships, and a cycle of sin that hinders our spiritual journey and our ability to reflect God's love to others.

One of the key lessons we can learn from the angry man is the importance of self-control in our spiritual life. Proverbs 14:17 emphasizes that those who are "soon angry" act foolishly, highlighting the need for self-control in managing our emotions. In our walk with the Lord, we must be vigilant in recognizing the triggers of our anger and take proactive steps to control it. This might involve prayer, seeking counsel, or simply taking a moment to pause and reflect before reacting. By exercising self-control, we can prevent anger from leading us into sin and can respond to situations with wisdom and grace. The angry man's example challenges us to be intentional about managing our emotions, knowing that self-control is a fruit of the Spirit that reflects our commitment to living a life that honors God.

Another important lesson from the angry man is the value of choosing our relationships wisely. Proverbs 22:24's warning against forming close ties with an angry person reminds us that the people we surround ourselves with can greatly influence our behavior and our spiritual growth. In our walk with the Lord, we must seek out relationships that encourage us to grow in patience, understanding, and love, rather than those that pull us into cycles of anger and conflict. This doesn't mean we should avoid those who struggle with anger altogether, but we should be mindful of the impact that close relationships with angry individuals can have on our own spiritual health. By surrounding ourselves with people who embody the qualities of peace and wisdom, we can create an environment that fosters spiritual growth and reflects the love of Christ.

The angry man's tendency to stir up strife, as described in Proverbs 29:22, also teaches us about the importance of being peacemakers in our relationships. The angry man's inability to control his temper leads to conflict and division, creating an atmosphere of tension and discord. In our walk with the Lord, we are called to be peacemakers, to seek reconciliation and to work towards harmony in our relationships. This means being willing to address conflicts in a constructive and loving manner, rather than allowing anger to fester and escalate into more serious issues. The angry man's example challenges us to be proactive in resolving conflicts, to practice forgiveness, and to strive for peace in all our interactions. By doing so, we can create relationships that are built on a foundation of mutual respect, understanding, and love, reflecting the peace that God desires for His people.

In conclusion, the angry man in Proverbs 14:17, 22:24, and 29:22 provides us with valuable lessons that are essential for our walk with the Lord. His life serves as a powerful warning of the dangers of uncontrolled anger, the importance of self-control, and the value of cultivating relationships that promote peace and spiritual growth. The angry man's quick temper, impulsive actions, and tendency to stir up strife lead to a life marked by turmoil and division, but his story also offers important insights into how we can manage our emotions in a way that honors God. By learning from the angry man's mistakes, we can embrace the qualities of patience, self-control, and peace, and work towards building relationships that reflect God's love and grace. The angry man's story is a reminder that while anger is a natural emotion, it must be managed carefully and channeled in ways that align with God's will. In our walk with the Lord, we must strive to be slow to anger, to seek peace in our relationships, and to respond to challenges with wisdom and grace. By doing so, we can prevent anger from leading us into sin and can live a life that reflects the love, patience, and forgiveness that God extends to each of us. Through the practice of self-control and the pursuit of peace, we can build relationships that are characterized by understanding, harmony, and mutual respect, and we can experience the fullness of life that God promises to those who seek to live in accordance with His wisdom and righteousness.

Chapter 12 – The Rich Man

Proverbs 10:15, "The rich man's wealth is his strong city: the destruction of the poor is their poverty," Proverbs 18:11, "The rich man's wealth is his strong city, and as an high wall in his own conceit," and Proverbs 28:11, "The rich man is wise in his own conceit; but the poor that hath understanding searcheth him out," provide a compelling and insightful look at the rich man as described in the book of Proverbs. The rich man, according to these verses, often places his trust and sense of security in his wealth, viewing it as a fortress that protects him from the difficulties and challenges of life. However, this reliance on material wealth can lead to a false sense of security and a prideful attitude that ultimately blinds him to the deeper, more meaningful aspects of life and spirituality. The rich man's life, as portrayed in these proverbs, serves as both a caution and a lesson about the dangers of trusting in wealth and the importance of humility, wisdom, and a proper understanding of the true source of security and fulfillment. The lessons one can learn from the rich man in Proverbs are crucial for our walk with the Lord, as they teach us the importance of placing our trust in God rather than in material possessions, the value of humility over pride, and the need to seek true wisdom that comes from understanding God's ways.

Proverbs 10:15 presents the rich man's wealth as a "strong city," suggesting that he sees his financial resources as a form of protection and security. For the rich man, wealth is more than just a means to acquire goods and services; it is a shield that he believes can protect him from the uncertainties and adversities of life. This "strong city" metaphor implies that the rich man views his wealth as impenetrable, something that can keep him safe from the struggles that others face. However, this perception can be dangerously misleading. While wealth can indeed provide certain comforts and protections, it is not a foolproof safeguard against all of life's challenges, particularly those of a spiritual or emotional nature. In our walk with the Lord, this teaches us that while wealth can be a blessing, it should not be the foundation of our security or identity. The rich man's reliance on his wealth as his "strong city" serves as a warning that material possessions can create a false sense of security that distracts us from our need for God and His protection. True security comes not from wealth but from a deep and abiding relationship with God, who is our ultimate fortress and refuge. By placing our trust in Him rather than in material wealth, we can navigate life's challenges with a sense of peace and assurance that no amount of money can provide.

Proverbs 18:11 reinforces this idea by describing the rich man's wealth as "a high wall in his own conceit." This verse highlights the pride and self-sufficiency that often accompany great wealth. The rich man, seeing his wealth as a high wall, believes that he is invulnerable to the difficulties that others face. This "high wall" symbolizes not just protection but also separation—wealth can create a barrier that isolates the rich man from the realities of life, from the struggles of others, and from the humility that comes from recognizing our dependence on God. The phrase "in his own conceit" emphasizes that this perception is rooted in pride, a dangerous self-deception that blinds the rich man to his own vulnerabilities and to the true nature of security. In our walk with the Lord, this teaches us the importance of humility and the dangers of pride. The rich man's belief in the invincibility of his wealth serves as a cautionary tale about the perils of self-reliance and the false sense of superiority that can accompany material success. True wisdom comes from recognizing that wealth is fleeting and that our true strength and security come from God alone. By cultivating humility and acknowledging our need for God, we can avoid the pitfalls of pride and maintain a perspective that keeps us grounded in the reality of our dependence on Him.

Proverbs 28:11 adds another layer to this discussion by contrasting the rich man's self-perceived wisdom with the understanding of the poor: "The rich man is wise in his own conceit; but the poor that hath understanding searcheth him out." This verse highlights the tendency of the rich man to believe that his wealth automatically confers wisdom upon him. In his "own conceit," the rich man sees himself as wise because of his success and financial acumen. However, this verse also suggests that this self-perceived wisdom is superficial and often flawed. The poor man, who lacks wealth but possesses true understanding, is able to see through the rich man's conceit and recognize the limitations of his wisdom. This contrast underscores the idea that true wisdom is not dependent on wealth but on a deeper understanding of life, spirituality, and the ways of God. In our walk with the Lord, this teaches us that we should not equate financial success with wisdom or assume that wealth automatically makes someone more insightful or knowledgeable. True wisdom comes from a heart that seeks God, that understands the deeper truths of life, and that is open to learning and growing in humility and understanding. The rich man's story serves as a reminder that wealth can be a distraction from true wisdom, leading us to rely on our own understanding rather than seeking God's guidance. By prioritizing spiritual wisdom over material success, we can develop a deeper relationship with God and gain the understanding that leads to a truly fulfilling and meaningful life.

The life of the rich man, as described in these proverbs, serves as a powerful example of the potential pitfalls of wealth and the importance of maintaining a proper perspective on material possessions. The rich man's reliance on his wealth as a source of security, his prideful belief in his own wisdom, and his isolation from the realities of life all highlight the dangers of placing too much value on material success. While wealth can provide certain comforts and opportunities, it is not a substitute for the deeper security and fulfillment that come from a relationship with God. The rich man's story is not just a cautionary tale about the dangers of wealth but also a call to seek true wisdom and understanding, to cultivate humility, and to place our trust in God rather than in material possessions.

One of the key lessons we can learn from the rich man is the importance of recognizing the limitations of wealth and the need to place our trust in God. Proverbs 10:15's depiction of wealth as a "strong city" serves as a reminder that while money can provide temporary security, it is not a reliable foundation for our lives. In our walk with the Lord, we must be careful not to allow wealth to become our primary source of security or identity. Instead, we should place our trust in God, who is our true refuge and strength. By keeping our focus on God rather than on material possessions, we can avoid the false sense of security that wealth can create and maintain a sense of peace and assurance that is grounded in our relationship with Him.

Another important lesson from the rich man is the value of humility and the dangers of pride. Proverbs 18:11's warning about the rich man's "high wall" of conceit highlights the risk of becoming prideful and self-reliant when we have material success. In our walk with the Lord, we must strive to cultivate humility, recognizing that all we have comes from God and that we are dependent on Him for our true security and wisdom. The rich man's story serves as a caution against allowing wealth to lead us into pride and self-deception. Instead, we should remain humble, acknowledging our need for God and seeking His guidance in all areas of our lives.

The contrast between the rich man's self-perceived wisdom and the understanding of the poor in Proverbs 28:11 also teaches us about the true source of wisdom. In our walk with the Lord, we should not equate financial success with wisdom or assume that wealth automatically makes someone more knowledgeable or insightful. True wisdom comes from a heart that seeks God, that is open to learning, and that understands the deeper truths of life and spirituality. The rich man's story reminds us that wealth can be a distraction from true wisdom, leading us to rely on our own understanding rather than seeking God's guidance. By prioritizing spiritual wisdom and understanding over material success, we can develop a deeper relationship with God and gain the insight that leads to a truly fulfilling and meaningful life.

In conclusion, the rich man in Proverbs 10:15, 18:11, and 28:11 provides us with valuable lessons that are essential for our walk with the Lord. His life serves as a powerful reminder of the potential pitfalls of wealth and the importance of maintaining a proper perspective on material possessions. The rich man's reliance on his wealth as a source of security, his prideful belief in his own wisdom, and his isolation from the realities of life all highlight the dangers of placing too much value on material success. By learning from the rich man's example, we can avoid the false sense of security that wealth can create, cultivate humility, and seek true wisdom that comes from understanding God's ways. The rich man's story is not just a cautionary tale about the dangers of wealth but also a call to seek a deeper relationship with God, to trust in Him rather than in material possessions, and to prioritize spiritual wisdom over worldly success. In our walk with the Lord, we must strive to keep our focus on God, recognizing that true security and fulfillment come from our relationship with Him, not from the accumulation of wealth. By doing so, we can experience the peace, wisdom, and understanding that lead to a life that is truly rich in the things that matter most.

Chapter 13 – The Poor Man

Proverbs 10:15, "The rich man's wealth is his strong city: the destruction of the poor is their poverty," Proverbs 13:7, "There is that maketh himself rich, yet hath nothing: there is that maketh himself poor, yet hath great riches," and Proverbs 19:7, "All the brethren of the poor do hate him: how much more do his friends go far from him? he pursueth them with words, yet they are wanting to him," provide a thought-provoking and poignant portrayal of the poor man as described in the book of Proverbs. The poor man is often seen through the lens of his lack of material wealth, but these verses reveal deeper truths about the spiritual and relational aspects of poverty. While the poor man may suffer from the physical and social challenges that come with financial lack, there are lessons and insights to be gained from his experience that can be invaluable in our walk with the Lord. The poor man's life serves as both a reflection on the difficulties of poverty and a reminder of the greater riches that can be found in spiritual wealth and a relationship with God. The lessons one can learn from the poor man in Proverbs are essential for understanding the limitations of material wealth, the value of humility, the importance of community and support, and the recognition that true riches are not measured in earthly possessions but in one's connection with God and others.

Proverbs 10:15 highlights the stark contrast between the rich man's sense of security in his wealth and the poor man's vulnerability: "The rich man's wealth is his strong city: the destruction of the poor is their poverty." This verse underscores the reality that poverty can bring about significant challenges and hardships, making life more difficult and uncertain. For the rich man, wealth acts as a "strong city," a metaphorical fortress that provides protection and security from many of life's troubles. In contrast, the poor man's lack of resources leaves him exposed and vulnerable, without the same means to shield himself from adversity. This comparison might seem discouraging at first glance, but it also serves as a reminder of the limitations of wealth and the true source of security. In our walk with the Lord, this teaches us that while poverty can indeed bring challenges, it also highlights the need to seek security in something more enduring than material wealth. The poor man's vulnerability points us toward the understanding that true security comes from God, who is our ultimate refuge and strength. Unlike wealth, which can be fleeting and uncertain, God's protection and provision are steadfast and eternal. By placing our trust in God rather than in material wealth, we can find peace and assurance even in the face of financial difficulties, knowing that our true worth and security are found in Him.

Proverbs 13:7 presents a paradoxical truth about wealth and poverty: "There is that maketh himself rich, yet hath nothing: there is that maketh himself poor, yet hath great riches." This verse challenges the conventional view of wealth by suggesting that material riches do not necessarily equate to true wealth. A person may accumulate great wealth and yet find themselves lacking in the things that truly matter, such as peace, joy, love, and a meaningful relationship with God. On the other hand, a person who appears poor in material terms may possess great spiritual wealth, characterized by contentment, a deep connection with God, and the richness of relationships with others. In our walk with the Lord, this teaches us that true riches are not found in the accumulation of material possessions but in the richness of our spiritual life and our relationships. The poor man, though lacking in earthly wealth, may be rich in faith, wisdom, and the qualities that bring true fulfillment. This verse encourages us to reevaluate our understanding of wealth and to focus on cultivating the riches that cannot be measured in dollars and cents but are of eternal value. By seeking to grow in our relationship with God and to build meaningful connections with others, we can experience the kind of wealth that brings lasting satisfaction and joy, regardless of our financial situation.

Proverbs 19:7 sheds light on the social challenges that often accompany poverty: "All the brethren of the poor do hate him: how much more do his friends go far from him? he pursueth them with words, yet they are wanting to him." This verse poignantly illustrates the isolation and rejection that the poor man may experience, even from those who should be closest to him. Poverty can lead to social stigma, where the poor man is shunned or neglected by his family and friends, leaving him to face his struggles alone. This lack of support and companionship can be one of the most painful aspects of poverty, compounding the difficulties of financial hardship with the emotional burden of loneliness and rejection. In our walk with the Lord, this teaches us the importance of compassion, community, and support for those who are struggling. The poor man's experience of isolation serves as a reminder that we are called to be a source of encouragement and help to those in need, reflecting God's love and care through our actions. It challenges us to reach out to those who may be marginalized or overlooked, offering friendship, support, and practical assistance. By doing so, we can help to alleviate the burden of poverty and bring hope and comfort to those who are struggling. Moreover, the poor man's experience also reminds us of the value of community and the importance of not allowing material circumstances to dictate the worth or dignity of a person. In God's eyes, every individual is valuable and deserving of love and respect, regardless of their financial situation.

The life of the poor man, as described in these proverbs, serves as a powerful reflection on the nature of wealth, the challenges of poverty, and the importance of finding true security and worth in God. His experience reveals the limitations of material wealth and the ways in which poverty can lead to vulnerability, social isolation, and a reevaluation of what it means to be truly rich. The poor man's story is not just a lament about the difficulties of financial lack but also a call to recognize the deeper, spiritual riches that can be found in a life lived in relationship with God. His life challenges us to reconsider our values, to place less emphasis on material possessions, and to seek the wealth that comes from knowing and serving God.

One of the key lessons we can learn from the poor man is the importance of finding our security in God rather than in material wealth. Proverbs 10:15's contrast between the rich man's "strong city" and the poor man's "destruction" serves as a reminder that while wealth can provide temporary security, it is ultimately unreliable and insufficient. In our walk with the Lord, we must place our trust in God, who is our true refuge and strength. By relying on God rather than on our financial resources, we can find peace and assurance even in times of financial difficulty, knowing that God will provide for our needs and protect us from harm. The poor man's experience teaches us to depend on God for our security and to trust in His provision, regardless of our material circumstances.

Another important lesson from the poor man is the value of spiritual wealth over material riches. Proverbs 13:7 challenges the conventional view of wealth by suggesting that true riches are not measured in material possessions but in the qualities of the heart and soul. In our walk with the Lord, we must prioritize the pursuit of spiritual wealth, seeking to grow in our relationship with God and to develop the qualities that bring true fulfillment and joy. The poor man's example reminds us that even if we lack material wealth, we can still be rich in faith, wisdom, love, and the things that matter most. By focusing on spiritual growth and cultivating a life of faith, we can experience the kind of wealth that brings lasting satisfaction and joy, transcending the ups and downs of our financial situation.

The poor man's experience of social isolation, as described in Proverbs 19:7, also teaches us about the importance of compassion and community. Poverty can lead to loneliness and rejection, but as followers of Christ, we are called to be a source of support and encouragement to those who are struggling. In our walk with the Lord, we must be mindful of those who may be marginalized or overlooked because of their financial situation, and we should seek to offer friendship, support, and practical assistance. By reaching out to those in need, we can reflect God's love and care, helping to alleviate the burden of poverty and bringing hope and comfort to those who are struggling. The poor man's experience challenges us to build a community that values and supports every individual, regardless of their material circumstances, and to recognize the inherent worth and dignity of every person in God's eyes.

In conclusion, the poor man in Proverbs 10:15, 13:7, and 19:7 provides us with valuable lessons that are essential for our walk with the Lord. His life serves as a powerful reflection on the limitations of material wealth, the challenges of poverty, and the importance of finding true security and worth in God. The poor man's vulnerability, his experience of social isolation, and his paradoxical richness in spiritual terms all highlight the need to place less emphasis on material possessions and to seek the deeper, spiritual riches that come from a relationship with God. By learning from the poor man's example, we can avoid the trap of placing our security in wealth, cultivate spiritual wealth that brings true fulfillment, and build a community that reflects God's love and compassion for all people. The poor man's story is not just a lament about the difficulties of poverty but also a call to recognize the greater riches that can be found in a life lived in relationship with God. In our walk with the Lord, we must strive to prioritize spiritual growth over material success, to depend on God for our security, and to extend love and support to those who are struggling. By doing so, we can experience the peace, joy, and fulfillment that come from knowing and serving God, and we can help to create a world where every individual is valued and supported, regardless of their financial situation. The poor man's story serves as a reminder that true wealth is not measured in dollars and cents but in the richness of our relationship with God and others, and that even in the face of financial challenges, we can find hope, peace, and purpose in our walk with the Lord.

Chapter 14 – The Evil Man

Proverbs 2:12, "To deliver thee from the way of the evil man, from the man that speaketh froward things," Proverbs 4:14, "Enter not into the path of the wicked, and go not in the way of evil men," and Proverbs 24:1, "Be not thou envious against evil men, neither desire to be with them," offer a stark and sobering depiction of the evil man as described in the book of Proverbs. The evil man is characterized by his deliberate choice to walk in ways that are contrary to God's commands, his use of deceptive and harmful speech, and his persistent pursuit of wickedness. Unlike the righteous man who seeks to live according to God's principles, the evil man intentionally chooses a path that leads away from goodness, truth, and righteousness. His life is marked by a pattern of destructive behavior, a hardened heart, and a deep-rooted resistance to the wisdom and guidance that come from God. The lessons one can learn from the evil man in Proverbs are crucial for our walk with the Lord, as they teach us the importance of discernment, the necessity of avoiding the influence of evil, and the value of staying committed to the path of righteousness.

Proverbs 2:12 warns of the dangers posed by the evil man and highlights the importance of being delivered from his influence: "To deliver thee from the way of the evil man, from the man that speaketh froward things." This verse emphasizes the need for divine protection and guidance to avoid being led astray by those who deliberately choose to do wrong. The evil man is not merely someone who occasionally makes mistakes or falls into sin; he is someone who actively engages in behavior that is twisted, perverse, and contrary to God's will. His speech is described as "froward," meaning that it is deceitful, rebellious, and aimed at leading others into error. The evil man's words are designed to distort the truth and to draw others into the same path of wickedness that he follows. In our walk with the Lord, this teaches us the importance of being vigilant and discerning in our relationships and interactions with others. We must be aware of the influence that the words and actions of others can have on us, and we must seek God's wisdom and protection to avoid being drawn into the ways of the evil man. By staying close to God, immersing ourselves in His Word, and seeking the guidance of the Holy Spirit, we can be delivered from the influence of evil and remain steadfast in our commitment to righteousness.

Proverbs 4:14 offers a clear and direct command to avoid the path of the evil man: "Enter not into the path of the wicked, and go not in the way of evil men." This verse provides a strong warning against even beginning to walk in the way of evil. The use of the word "enter" suggests that there is a choice to be made, a decision about whether to step onto a path that leads away from God's ways and towards wickedness. The instruction to "go not in the way of evil men" emphasizes the importance of making deliberate choices to avoid situations, influences, and behaviors that could lead us away from righteousness. The path of the wicked is one that ultimately leads to destruction, both spiritually and, often, physically. In our walk with the Lord, this teaches us the importance of making wise and intentional choices about the paths we choose to walk on. We must be vigilant in avoiding anything that could lead us away from God, whether it be certain relationships, habits, or environments that are conducive to sinful behavior. By choosing to walk in the path of righteousness, we align ourselves with God's will and position ourselves to receive His guidance, protection, and blessings. The evil man's example serves as a reminder that the choices we make have significant consequences, and that we must be careful to choose the path that leads to life and not to destruction.

Proverbs 24:1 adds another layer of insight by warning against envying or desiring the company of evil men: "Be not thou envious against evil men, neither desire to be with them." This verse addresses a common temptation that many people face: the temptation to envy the apparent success, power, or pleasure that evil men seem to enjoy. The world often glorifies those who achieve success through unethical or sinful means, and it can be tempting to desire the same prosperity or status. However, Proverbs 24:1 cautions us against falling into this trap, reminding us that the success of the evil man is fleeting and ultimately leads to destruction. The verse also warns against the desire to associate with evil men, recognizing that such associations can have a corrupting influence on our own character and spiritual life. In our walk with the Lord, this teaches us the importance of keeping our eyes fixed on God's standards and not being swayed by the false allure of worldly success. We must resist the temptation to envy those who achieve their goals through ungodly means and instead focus on living a life that is pleasing to God, knowing that true success is found in faithfulness to Him. The evil man's example serves as a warning that the temporary rewards of wickedness are not worth the long-term consequences, and that we must be content with the blessings that come from walking in righteousness, even if they are not as immediately apparent or celebrated by the world.

The life of the evil man, as described in these proverbs, serves as a powerful example of the consequences of choosing a path that is contrary to God's will. His deliberate engagement in wickedness, his use of deceitful and harmful speech, and his apparent success in the world all lead to a life that is ultimately empty, destructive, and separated from God. The evil man's life is marked by a pattern of behavior that not only harms others but also leads to his own downfall. His story is not just a cautionary tale about the dangers of wickedness, but also a reminder of the importance of staying committed to the path of righteousness, regardless of the temptations and challenges we may face.

One of the key lessons we can learn from the evil man is the importance of discernment and vigilance in our spiritual life. Proverbs 2:12's warning about the influence of the evil man's "froward" speech highlights the need for us to be discerning in the voices we listen to and the influences we allow into our lives. In our walk with the Lord, we must be careful to surround ourselves with people, teachings, and environments that encourage us to grow in our faith and to live according to God's principles. We must also be vigilant in recognizing and rejecting the deceptive and harmful influences that seek to lead us away from God. By staying rooted in God's Word and seeking the guidance of the Holy Spirit, we can develop the discernment needed to recognize the ways of the evil man and to avoid being drawn into them.

Another important lesson from the evil man is the necessity of making deliberate choices to avoid the path of wickedness. Proverbs 4:14's command to "enter not into the path of the wicked" emphasizes that we have a choice in the paths we take in life. In our walk with the Lord, we must be intentional about choosing the path of righteousness and avoiding anything that could lead us away from God's will. This means being mindful of the relationships we form, the habits we cultivate, and the environments we engage with. By choosing to walk in the path of righteousness, we position ourselves to receive God's guidance, protection, and blessings, and we avoid the destructive consequences that come from walking in the way of evil.

The warning in Proverbs 24:1 against envying or desiring the company of evil men also teaches us about the importance of contentment and focusing on God's standards rather than worldly success. In our walk with the Lord, we must resist the temptation to envy those who achieve success through ungodly means and instead focus on living a life that is pleasing to God. The evil man's apparent success is ultimately hollow and short-lived, while the rewards of righteousness are lasting and deeply fulfilling. By keeping our eyes fixed on God and His standards, we can avoid the pitfalls of envy and remain committed to the path of righteousness, knowing that true success is found in faithfulness to Him.

In conclusion, the evil man in Proverbs 2:12, 4:14, and 24:1 provides us with valuable lessons that are essential for our walk with the Lord. His life serves as a powerful warning of the consequences of choosing a path that is contrary to God's will and the importance of staying committed to the path of righteousness. The evil man's deliberate engagement in wickedness, his use of deceitful and harmful speech, and his apparent success in the world all lead to a life that is ultimately empty, destructive, and separated from God. By learning from the evil man's example, we can develop the discernment needed to recognize and reject the influences of evil, make deliberate choices to avoid the path of wickedness, and focus on living a life that is pleasing to God. The evil man's story is not just a cautionary tale about the dangers of wickedness but also a reminder of the importance of staying committed to the path of righteousness, regardless of the temptations and challenges we may face. In our walk with the Lord, we must strive to remain vigilant, to surround ourselves with godly influences, and to keep our eyes fixed on God's standards rather than the fleeting success of the world. By doing so, we can avoid the destructive consequences of wickedness and experience the lasting peace, joy, and fulfillment that come from living a life that is aligned with God's will. The evil man's story serves as a reminder that the choices we make have significant consequences, and that by choosing the path of righteousness, we position ourselves to receive God's guidance, protection, and blessings, both in this life and in the life to come.

Chapter 15 – The Generous Man

Proverbs 11:25, "The liberal soul shall be made fat: and he that watereth shall be watered also himself," and Proverbs 22:9, "He that hath a bountiful eye shall be blessed; for he giveth of his bread to the poor," paint a rich and inspiring picture of the generous man as described in the book of Proverbs. The generous man is characterized by his willingness to share what he has, his open-heartedness, and his commitment to helping others. Unlike the stingy or self-centered individual who hoards resources for personal gain, the generous man recognizes the value of giving and the impact it has not only on those who receive but also on himself. His life is marked by a spirit of abundance, not just in terms of material wealth but in the richness of relationships, the joy of helping others, and the blessings that flow back to him as a result of his generosity. The generous man's example provides valuable lessons for our walk with the Lord, teaching us the importance of living with an open heart, the joy of giving, and the spiritual rewards that come from being a blessing to others.

Proverbs 11:25 emphasizes the principle of reciprocity in generosity: "The liberal soul shall be made fat: and he that watereth shall be watered also himself." This verse illustrates the concept that when we give to others, we often receive blessings in return. The phrase "liberal soul" refers to a person who is generous, willing to share their resources, whether it be time, money, or talents, with those in need. The result of this generosity is that the generous person becomes "fat," a metaphorical expression indicating abundance, prosperity, and well-being. Similarly, the one who "watereth" others, meaning the person who refreshes, supports, and nurtures those around them, will find that they themselves are refreshed and supported in return. In our walk with the Lord, this teaches us that generosity is not just about giving away what we have, but about participating in a cycle of blessing where our acts of kindness and support lead to our own spiritual and emotional enrichment. The generous man understands that in God's economy, the more we give, the more we receive—not necessarily in material terms, but in the richness of relationships, the depth of joy, and the satisfaction that comes from knowing we are making a positive difference in the lives of others. This verse challenges us to adopt a mindset of generosity, knowing that as we pour out into others, we too will be filled with the blessings that come from living a life of service and love.

Proverbs 22:9 further highlights the blessings that come to the generous man: "He that hath a bountiful eye shall be blessed; for he giveth of his bread to the poor." This verse focuses on the attitude and perspective of the generous person, describing him as someone with a "bountiful eye," meaning that he sees the world through the lens of abundance and opportunity rather than scarcity and fear. The generous man is not concerned with hoarding his resources or worrying about having enough for himself; instead, he is eager to share what he has with those in need. His generosity is not limited to grand gestures but is evident in his willingness to give even the basic necessities, such as "bread," to the poor. The result of this generosity is that the generous man is "blessed"—he experiences God's favor, protection, and provision in his life. In our walk with the Lord, this teaches us the importance of cultivating a bountiful eye, a perspective that sees opportunities to bless others rather than reasons to hold back. The generous man's example encourages us to trust in God's provision, knowing that when we give to others, God will take care of our needs. This verse also reminds us that true generosity comes from the heart and is reflected in our willingness to share even when we may not have an abundance. By giving with a bountiful eye, we align ourselves with God's heart for the poor and the needy, and we open ourselves up to the blessings that come from being a conduit of His love and provision.

The life of the generous man, as described in these proverbs, serves as a powerful example of the joy and fulfillment that come from living a life of giving and service. His generosity is not just about the act of giving but about the mindset and heart attitude that underlie his actions. The generous man sees the world as a place of abundance, where there is always enough to share, and he recognizes that by giving to others, he is participating in God's work of blessing and provision. His life is marked by the satisfaction of knowing that he is making a difference in the lives of others, and by the blessings that flow back to him as a result of his generosity. The generous man's story is not just an encouragement to give, but a call to adopt a lifestyle of generosity, where giving becomes a natural and joyful expression of our love for God and others.

One of the key lessons we can learn from the generous man is the importance of living with an open heart and a mindset of abundance. Proverbs 11:25's emphasis on the reciprocity of generosity teaches us that when we give, we often receive blessings in return. In our walk with the Lord, we must cultivate a heart that is willing to share what we have, whether it be our time, resources, or talents, with those in need. By doing so, we participate in a cycle of blessing where our acts of kindness lead to our own spiritual and emotional enrichment. The generous man's example challenges us to move beyond a mindset of scarcity and fear, and to embrace the joy of giving, knowing that God will provide for our needs as we care for others.

Another important lesson from the generous man is the value of seeing the world through a bountiful eye. Proverbs 22:9's description of the generous man as someone with a "bountiful eye" teaches us the importance of perspective in our giving. In our walk with the Lord, we must strive to see the world through the lens of abundance and opportunity, rather than scarcity and fear. The generous man's willingness to share even the basic necessities with the poor reflects a heart that trusts in God's provision and is eager to bless others. This verse challenges us to examine our own attitudes toward giving, and to cultivate a perspective that is open to sharing what we have, no matter how small, with those in need. By doing so, we align ourselves with God's heart for the poor and needy, and we open ourselves up to the blessings that come from being a channel of His love and provision.

The generous man's life also teaches us about the spiritual rewards of living a life of giving and service. Proverbs 11:25's reminder that "he that watereth shall be watered also himself" highlights the spiritual and emotional enrichment that comes from giving to others. In our walk with the Lord, we must recognize that generosity is not just about the material act of giving, but about the impact it has on our own hearts and souls. The generous man's willingness to pour into others leads to his own spiritual growth, deepening his connection with God and increasing his capacity for love and compassion. This verse challenges us to embrace generosity as a spiritual discipline, one that not only blesses others but also transforms our own hearts and brings us closer to God.

In conclusion, the generous man in Proverbs 11:25 and 22:9 provides us with valuable lessons that are essential for our walk with the Lord. His life serves as a powerful example of the joy, fulfillment, and spiritual growth that come from living a life of giving and service. The generous man's willingness to share what he has, his open-heartedness, and his commitment to helping others all highlight the importance of living with an open heart and a mindset of abundance. By learning from the generous man's example, we can embrace the joy of giving, trust in God's provision, and experience the spiritual rewards that come from being a blessing to others. The generous man's story is not just an encouragement to give, but a call to adopt a lifestyle of generosity, where giving becomes a natural and joyful expression of our love for God and others. In our walk with the Lord, we must strive to live with a bountiful eye, seeing the world as a place of abundance and opportunity, and recognizing that true wealth is found not in what we accumulate, but in what we give away. By doing so, we can experience the fullness of life that comes from living in alignment with God's heart for generosity, and we can be a source of blessing and encouragement to those around us. The generous man's life serves as a reminder that in God's economy, the more we give, the more we receive—not necessarily in material terms, but in the richness of relationships, the depth of joy, and the satisfaction that comes from knowing we are making a positive difference in the lives of others. By living a life of generosity, we reflect the character of God, who is the ultimate giver, and we open ourselves up to the abundant blessings that come from walking in His ways.

Chapter 16 – The Oppressed Man

Proverbs 14:31, "He that oppresseth the poor reproacheth his Maker: but he that honoureth him hath mercy on the poor," and Proverbs 28:3, "A poor man that oppresseth the poor is like a sweeping rain which leaveth no food," offer a vivid and thought-provoking depiction of the oppressed man and the dynamics of oppression as described in the book of Proverbs. The oppressed man is often seen as someone who suffers under the weight of injustice, exploitation, and mistreatment, particularly at the hands of those who have power and wealth. These verses reveal that oppression is not only a social or economic issue but also a deeply spiritual one that touches the heart of God. The way we treat the oppressed reflects our reverence (or lack thereof) for God Himself. The lessons one can learn from the experience of the oppressed man in Proverbs are crucial for our walk with the Lord, as they teach us about the importance of compassion, justice, the dangers of oppressing others, and the need for aligning our actions with God's heart for the vulnerable and marginalized.

Proverbs 14:31 begins by highlighting a powerful truth: "He that oppresseth the poor reproacheth his Maker." This statement reveals that when someone oppresses a poor or vulnerable person, they are not merely committing a social injustice—they are directly offending God, who is the Maker of all. The poor, like every human being, are made in the image of God, and to mistreat them is to show disregard for their inherent dignity and worth. Oppression in any form—whether it be economic exploitation, denial of justice, or social exclusion—is a direct insult to God because it disregards His command to love and care for our fellow human beings. In our walk with the Lord, this verse teaches us the importance of seeing each person, especially the poor and oppressed, as valuable in the eyes of God. It challenges us to examine our own actions and attitudes towards others, particularly those who are less fortunate, and to ensure that we are treating them with the respect, dignity, and compassion that God requires. The oppressed man's experience reminds us that God is deeply concerned with how we treat those who are vulnerable, and that our actions toward them are a reflection of our relationship with God Himself. By choosing to honor and help the oppressed, we are not only showing kindness to them but also demonstrating our reverence and love for God.

The second part of Proverbs 14:31 contrasts the behavior of the oppressor with that of the one who honors God: "But he that honoureth him hath mercy on the poor." This part of the verse emphasizes that honoring God is directly connected to showing mercy and compassion to the poor and oppressed. Mercy, in this context, is more than just feeling pity—it is about taking action to alleviate the suffering of those who are oppressed. The one who honors God recognizes that true worship and reverence for the Creator involve caring for His creation, particularly those who are most vulnerable. In our walk with the Lord, this verse teaches us that genuine faith is demonstrated through our actions, especially in how we treat those who are marginalized or suffering. It challenges us to move beyond mere words of faith and to live out our beliefs by actively working to bring justice and relief to the oppressed. The oppressed man's experience serves as a reminder that our worship of God is incomplete if it does not include acts of mercy and justice toward those in need. By showing mercy to the oppressed, we align ourselves with God's heart and participate in His work of bringing healing and restoration to a broken world.

Proverbs 28:3 offers a sobering warning about the dangers of oppression, particularly when it comes from someone who is also poor: "A poor man that oppresseth the poor is like a sweeping rain which leaveth no food." This verse paints a picture of devastation, comparing the actions of a poor oppressor to a "sweeping rain" that destroys crops and leaves nothing behind for sustenance. The imagery here is powerful—the idea that someone who has experienced poverty and hardship would turn around and oppress others in the same situation is seen as especially destructive and cruel. This kind of oppression is compared to a natural disaster that strips the land of its ability to produce food, leaving people even more vulnerable and destitute. In our walk with the Lord, this verse teaches us about the destructive nature of oppression, not only for the victims but also for the oppressor. It reminds us that power and wealth are not the only sources of oppression—sometimes, those who have suffered themselves can perpetuate cycles of injustice and exploitation when they gain even a small amount of power over others. The oppressed man's experience, therefore, is a call to break these cycles and to choose compassion and justice instead of continuing the patterns of oppression. It challenges us to examine how we use whatever influence or power we have, no matter how small, and to ensure that we are using it to uplift and support others rather than to harm or exploit them.

The life of the oppressed man, as described in these proverbs, serves as a powerful reflection on the dynamics of power, the importance of justice, and the spiritual implications of how we treat others. His experience reveals that oppression is not just a social issue but a deeply spiritual one that has serious consequences for our relationship with God. The oppressed man's story is not only a call to show compassion and mercy to those who are suffering but also a warning against the dangers of becoming an oppressor ourselves, even in small ways. His life challenges us to consider how we can be agents of justice and mercy in a world where oppression and inequality are all too common.

One of the key lessons we can learn from the oppressed man is the importance of recognizing the dignity and worth of every person, especially those who are marginalized or vulnerable. Proverbs 14:31's reminder that oppressing the poor is a reproach to God emphasizes that how we treat others, particularly those who are suffering, reflects our respect (or lack thereof) for God Himself. In our walk with the

Lord, we must be mindful of the ways in which we interact with others and ensure that our actions reflect the love, respect, and compassion that God requires of us. The oppressed man's experience teaches us that honoring God involves standing up for the rights and dignity of all people, and that our faith is demonstrated through our commitment to justice and mercy.

Another important lesson from the oppressed man is the need for active compassion and mercy. Proverbs 14:31's call to show mercy to the poor highlights that true worship of God involves more than just attending services or saying prayers—it requires us to take concrete actions to help those in need. In our walk with the Lord, we must be willing to step out of our comfort zones and engage with those who are suffering, offering not just words of comfort but also tangible support and assistance. The oppressed man's experience challenges us to live out our faith in practical ways, recognizing that our actions toward others are a reflection of our love for God. By showing mercy to the oppressed, we are participating in God's work of bringing healing and restoration to the world.

Proverbs 28:3's warning about the destructive nature of oppression, especially when it comes from those who have also experienced poverty, teaches us about the importance of breaking cycles of injustice. In our walk with the Lord, we must be vigilant in examining how we use whatever influence or power we have, ensuring that we are using it to uplift and support others rather than to perpetuate harm. The oppressed man's experience reminds us that even those who have suffered can become oppressors if they are not careful, and that true compassion involves breaking these cycles and choosing to act with justice and mercy. This verse challenges us to be mindful of our actions and to seek ways to be a positive force in the lives of others, using our resources, however limited, to bring relief and hope to those who are struggling.

In conclusion, the oppressed man in Proverbs 14:31 and 28:3 provides us with valuable lessons that are essential for our walk with the Lord. His life serves as a powerful reflection on the importance of compassion, justice, and the spiritual implications of how we treat others. The oppressed man's experience reveals that oppression is not just a social issue but a deeply spiritual one that touches the heart of God. By learning from the oppressed man's example, we can develop a greater awareness of the dignity and worth of every person, a commitment to active compassion and mercy, and a determination to break cycles of injustice and oppression in our own lives and communities. The oppressed man's story is not only a call to show mercy and support to those who are suffering but also a reminder of the dangers of becoming an oppressor ourselves, even in small ways. In our walk with the Lord, we must strive to be agents of justice and mercy, using whatever influence or power we have to uplift and support others rather than to harm or exploit them. By doing so, we can honor God, reflect His love and compassion to the world, and participate in His work of bringing healing and restoration to a broken world. The oppressed man's life serves as a reminder that true faith is demonstrated through our actions, especially in how we treat those who are most vulnerable, and that our relationship with God is deeply connected to our commitment to justice and mercy in the lives of others.

Chapter 17 – The Perverse Man

Proverbs 12:8, "A man shall be commended according to his wisdom: but he that is of a perverse heart shall be despised," Proverbs 14:2, "He that walketh in his uprightness feareth the Lord: but he that is perverse in his ways despiseth him," and Proverbs 16:28, "A froward man soweth strife: and a whisperer separateth chief friends," offer a vivid and cautionary portrayal of the perverse man as described in the book of Proverbs. The perverse man is characterized by his deliberate choice to embrace twisted and corrupt behavior, his rejection of righteousness, and his propensity to cause division and conflict among people. Unlike the upright man, who walks in the fear of the Lord and seeks to live according to God's principles, the perverse man actively chooses a path of moral corruption, deception, and hostility. His life is marked by a hardened heart, a disregard for God's ways, and a destructive influence on those around him. The lessons one can learn from the perverse man in Proverbs are crucial for our walk with the Lord, as they teach us about the dangers of embracing corruption, the importance of living with integrity, and the need to be vigilant against those who seek to sow discord and division.

Proverbs 12:8 begins by contrasting the commendation that comes with wisdom with the disdain that follows a perverse heart: "A man shall be commended according to his wisdom: but he that is of a perverse heart shall be despised." This verse emphasizes the value of wisdom and integrity, highlighting that those who live wisely and righteously are recognized and respected by others. In contrast, the perverse man, whose heart is twisted and corrupt, is despised because of his moral failures and the harm he causes. The term "perverse" refers to someone who deliberately chooses to deviate from what is right and good, embracing instead what is morally corrupt and harmful. The perverse man's actions are not only self-destructive but also damage his reputation and relationships, leading others to view him with contempt and mistrust. In our walk with the Lord, this verse teaches us the importance of guarding our hearts and minds against corruption. It challenges us to pursue wisdom and integrity, knowing that these qualities lead to a life of respect, honor, and positive influence. The perverse man's example serves as a warning that embracing corruption and moral compromise not only separates us from God but also alienates us from others, resulting in a life marked by isolation and disgrace. By choosing to live with integrity and wisdom, we align ourselves with God's will and position ourselves to be a blessing to others, building relationships based on trust, respect, and mutual honor.

Proverbs 14:2 further contrasts the upright man with the perverse man: "He that walketh in his uprightness feareth the Lord: but he that is perverse in his ways despiseth him." This verse highlights the connection between one's conduct and one's attitude toward God. The upright man, who walks in righteousness and integrity, does so because he has a deep reverence and fear of the Lord. His actions reflect his desire to honor God and live according to His commandments. In contrast, the perverse man's actions reveal his contempt for God. By choosing a path of moral corruption and wickedness, the perverse man demonstrates that he despises the Lord and rejects His authority. This verse underscores the idea that our behavior is a reflection of our relationship with God. In our walk with the Lord, this teaches us that living righteously and with integrity is not just about following rules but about expressing our love and respect for God. The perverse man's example serves as a reminder that when we choose to engage in sinful and corrupt behavior, we are not only harming ourselves and others but also showing disdain for God and His ways. To walk in uprightness is to live in a way that honors God and reflects His character, while choosing perversity is to reject God's authority and separate ourselves from His blessings. By cultivating a heart that fears and honors the Lord, we can ensure that our actions align with His will and that our lives are a testimony to His goodness and righteousness.

Proverbs 16:28 offers insight into the destructive impact of the perverse man's behavior on relationships: "A froward man soweth strife: and a whisperer separateth chief friends." This verse reveals that the perverse man, described here as "froward" or morally crooked, is a source of conflict and division. His actions and words are designed to create discord, stirring up strife among people and breaking apart even the closest of relationships. The term "whisperer" refers to someone who spreads gossip, slander, or false information in a secretive manner, causing misunderstandings and mistrust among friends. The perverse man's behavior is not only harmful to himself but also to the community around him, as his actions undermine unity and destroy the bonds of friendship and trust. In our walk with the Lord, this verse teaches us the importance of being peacemakers and maintaining integrity in our words and actions. The perverse man's example challenges us to be vigilant against the temptation to engage in gossip, slander, or any behavior that sows discord among others. Instead, we are called to be agents of peace, fostering harmony and unity in our relationships. By rejecting the ways of the perverse man and choosing to speak and act with integrity, we can build strong, healthy relationships that reflect God's love and promote the well-being of the community.

The life of the perverse man, as described in these proverbs, serves as a powerful example of the consequences of choosing a path of moral corruption, deception, and hostility. His deliberate rejection of righteousness and his embrace of perverse behavior lead to a life marked by isolation, conflict, and contempt from others. The perverse man's actions not only separate him from God but also from the respect and trust of those around him. His story is a sobering reminder of the destructive power of sin and the importance of living a life of integrity, wisdom, and reverence for God. The lessons we can learn from the perverse man are essential for understanding the importance of maintaining a pure heart, living with integrity, and being vigilant against the influence of those who seek to sow discord and division.

One of the key lessons we can learn from the perverse man is the importance of guarding our hearts and minds against corruption. Proverbs 12:8's contrast between the commendation that comes with wisdom and the disdain that follows a perverse heart highlights the value of living with integrity and moral uprightness. In our walk with the Lord, we must be diligent in pursuing wisdom, seeking to align our thoughts, words, and actions with God's will. The perverse man's example serves as a warning that embracing corruption and moral compromise not only leads to personal destruction but also alienates us from others, resulting in a life marked by isolation and disgrace. By choosing to live with integrity, we can build a life of respect, honor, and positive influence, reflecting God's character in all that we do.

Another important lesson from the perverse man is the connection between our conduct and our relationship with God. Proverbs 14:2's emphasis on the upright man's fear of the Lord and the perverse man's disdain for God teaches us that our behavior is a reflection of our attitude toward God. In our walk with the Lord, we must strive to live righteously and with integrity, not just out of a sense of duty, but as an expression of our love and reverence for God. The perverse man's example reminds us that when we choose to engage in sinful and corrupt behavior, we are not only harming ourselves and others but also rejecting God's authority and separating ourselves from His blessings. By cultivating a heart that fears and honors the Lord, we can ensure that our actions align with His will and that our lives are a testimony to His goodness and righteousness.

The destructive impact of the perverse man's behavior on relationships, as described in Proverbs 16:28, also teaches us about the importance of being peacemakers and maintaining integrity in our words and actions. The perverse man's tendency to sow strife and division serves as a warning against the dangers of gossip, slander, and any behavior that undermines unity and trust. In our walk with the Lord, we must be vigilant in guarding our speech and actions, choosing to promote peace and harmony in our relationships rather than conflict and division. The perverse man's example challenges us to reject the ways of deception and hostility and to embrace the call to be agents of peace, building strong, healthy relationships that reflect God's love and promote the well-being of the community.

In conclusion, the perverse man in Proverbs 12:8, 14:2, and 16:28 provides us with valuable lessons that are essential for our walk with the Lord. His life serves as a powerful warning of the consequences of choosing a path of moral corruption, deception, and hostility. The perverse man's deliberate rejection of righteousness and his embrace of perverse behavior lead to a life marked by isolation, conflict, and contempt from others. By learning from the perverse man's example, we can develop a greater awareness of the importance of guarding our hearts and minds against corruption, living with integrity, and being vigilant against those who seek to sow discord and division. The perverse man's story is not just a cautionary tale about the dangers of sin but also a call to pursue wisdom, integrity, and righteousness in our daily lives. In our walk with the Lord, we must strive to live in a way that honors God, reflects His character, and promotes peace and harmony in our relationships. By doing so, we can avoid the destructive consequences of perversity and experience the blessings of a life lived in alignment with God's will. The perverse man's life serves as a reminder that the choices we make have significant consequences, and that by choosing to walk in integrity, wisdom, and reverence for God, we position ourselves to receive His guidance, protection, and blessings, both in this life and in the life to come.

Chapter 18 – The Faithful Man

Proverbs 20:6, "Most men will proclaim every one his own goodness: but a faithful man who can find?" and Proverbs 28:20, "A faithful man shall abound with blessings: but he that maketh haste to be rich shall not be innocent," paint a compelling picture of the faithful man as described in the book of Proverbs. The faithful man is characterized by his unwavering commitment, reliability, and steadfastness in both his relationships and his duties. Unlike those who boast of their own goodness or seek quick and easy paths to success, the faithful man remains true to his word, consistent in his actions, and devoted to doing what is right, even when it is difficult. His life is marked by integrity, loyalty, and a deep sense of responsibility. The faithful man's example provides valuable lessons for our walk with the Lord, teaching us the importance of living a life of integrity, the value of faithfulness in all areas of our lives, and the blessings that come from being steadfast and trustworthy.

Proverbs 20:6 begins with an observation about human nature: "Most men will proclaim every one his own goodness." This part of the verse highlights the tendency of people to boast about their virtues, to speak highly of their own moral character, and to make themselves appear better than they actually are. It is easy for someone to declare themselves good, honest, or reliable, but words alone do not make a person truly virtuous. The verse then poses a rhetorical question that underscores the rarity of true faithfulness: "But a faithful man who can find?" This question suggests that while many may claim to be good, finding someone who is genuinely faithful—who consistently lives out their commitments and remains steadfast in their integrity—is much more difficult. Faithfulness, in this context, is not just about being loyal in relationships, but about a broader commitment to living with integrity, honesty, and reliability in all areas of life. In our walk with the Lord, this verse teaches us the importance of striving to be faithful in our actions, not just in our words. It challenges us to go beyond simply professing our faith or our goodness, and to demonstrate these qualities through consistent, reliable, and trustworthy behavior. The faithful man's example reminds us that true faithfulness is about living out our values and commitments every day, even when it is challenging or inconvenient.

Proverbs 28:20 adds to this understanding of faithfulness by highlighting the rewards that come with it: "A faithful man shall abound with blessings: but he that maketh haste to be rich shall not be innocent." This verse contrasts the faithful man with those who seek to gain wealth quickly, often through dishonest or unethical means. The faithful man is described as someone who "shall abound with blessings," indicating that his life is filled with the rewards that come from living with integrity, reliability, and steadfastness. These blessings may not always be material, but they include the respect and trust of others, a clear conscience, and a deep sense of fulfillment and peace. In contrast, those who prioritize quick wealth over faithfulness often find themselves entangled in sin and corruption, leading to guilt and regret. The verse suggests that the pursuit of riches through dishonest means ultimately leads to ruin, while faithfulness leads to lasting rewards. In our walk with the Lord, this verse teaches us the importance of prioritizing faithfulness over worldly success. The faithful man's example encourages us to remain committed to our values and responsibilities, even when it seems easier or more profitable to take shortcuts. By choosing to be faithful, we position ourselves to receive the blessings that come from living a life of integrity and trustworthiness, both in this life and in the life to come.

The life of the faithful man, as described in these proverbs, serves as a powerful example of the importance of integrity, reliability, and steadfastness in our spiritual journey. His unwavering commitment to doing what is right, his consistent behavior, and his loyalty in relationships all highlight the value of living with faithfulness. The faithful man does not seek recognition or praise for his actions; instead, he is motivated by a deep sense of responsibility and a desire to honor God in all that he does. His life is marked by the blessings that come from living in alignment with God's will, including the respect and trust of others, a clear conscience, and a profound sense of inner peace and fulfillment. The faithful man's story is not just an encouragement to be reliable and trustworthy, but a call to live out our faith in practical, everyday ways that reflect God's character and values.

One of the key lessons we can learn from the faithful man is the importance of living with integrity and consistency. Proverbs 20:6's observation about the rarity of true faithfulness challenges us to examine our own lives and ask whether our actions align with our words. In our walk with the Lord, we must strive to be faithful in all areas of our lives, whether it be in our relationships, our work, or our commitments to God. The faithful man's example teaches us that true faithfulness is not about making grand declarations of our goodness, but about living out our values every day, even in the small and seemingly insignificant details of life. By choosing to be faithful, we build a life of integrity that honors God and earns the trust and respect of others.

Another important lesson from the faithful man is the value of patience and steadfastness in the face of challenges. Proverbs 28:20's promise that the faithful man "shall abound with blessings" reminds us that the rewards of faithfulness are often not immediate but are the result of a lifetime of consistent, reliable behavior. In our walk with the Lord, we must be willing to endure difficulties and setbacks, knowing that our faithfulness will ultimately be rewarded. The faithful man's example encourages us to remain steadfast in our commitments, even when it would be easier to take shortcuts or abandon our responsibilities. By being faithful, we position ourselves to receive the blessings that come from living a life of integrity, including the deep sense of fulfillment and peace that comes from knowing we have done what is right.

The contrast between the faithful man and those who seek quick wealth through dishonest means, as described in Proverbs 28:20, also teaches us about the importance of prioritizing faithfulness over worldly success. In our walk with the Lord, we must be careful not to be seduced by the allure of quick and easy paths to success, especially when they involve compromising our values or integrity. The faithful man's example challenges us to focus on what truly matters—living a life that honors God, being reliable and trustworthy, and maintaining our integrity in all that we do. By choosing to be faithful rather than chasing after worldly success, we position ourselves to receive the lasting rewards that come from living in alignment with God's will.

In conclusion, the faithful man in Proverbs 20:6 and 28:20 provides us with valuable lessons that are essential for our walk with the Lord. His life serves as a powerful example of the importance of integrity, reliability, and steadfastness in all areas of life. The faithful man's unwavering commitment to doing what is right, his consistent behavior, and his loyalty in relationships all highlight the value of living with faithfulness. By learning from the faithful man's example, we can develop a greater awareness of the importance of living with integrity, remaining steadfast in our commitments, and prioritizing faithfulness over worldly success. The faithful man's story is not just an encouragement to be reliable and trustworthy, but a call to live out our faith in practical, everyday ways that reflect God's character and values. In our walk with the Lord, we must strive

Chapter 19 – The Violent Man

Proverbs 3:31, "Envy thou not the oppressor, and choose none of his ways," and Proverbs 16:29, "A violent man enticeth his neighbor, and leadeth him into the way that is not good," provide a stark and cautionary picture of the violent man as described in the book of Proverbs. The violent man is characterized by his use of force, intimidation, and aggression to achieve his ends, often at the expense of others. Unlike those who pursue peace, justice, and righteousness, the violent man seeks to impose his will through coercion and fear, disregarding the well-being of those around him. His life is marked by strife, conflict, and a disregard for the principles of love, kindness, and respect that are central to a life lived in accordance with God's will. The violent man's actions not only harm others but also lead him down a path of spiritual and moral decay. The lessons one can learn from the violent man in Proverbs are crucial for our walk with the Lord, as they teach us about the dangers of embracing aggression, the importance of pursuing peace and justice, and the need to resist the temptation to respond to conflict with violence or hostility.

Proverbs 3:31 begins with a direct command: "Envy thou not the oppressor, and choose none of his ways." This verse warns against the temptation to admire or emulate those who use force and violence to achieve their goals. The term "oppressor" refers to someone who uses their power to dominate and control others, often through violent or coercive means. The verse cautions against envying such individuals, who may appear successful or powerful in the eyes of the world but whose methods are fundamentally opposed to the values of righteousness and justice that God calls us to uphold. The second part of the verse, "choose none of his ways," reinforces the idea that we should actively reject the behaviors and tactics of the violent man. In our walk with the Lord, this verse teaches us the importance of resisting the allure of power that comes through violence or intimidation. It challenges us to recognize that true strength lies not in the ability to dominate others but in the ability to act with integrity, compassion, and respect for the dignity of all people. The violent man's example serves as a warning that the pursuit of power through force leads to a life of conflict, isolation, and spiritual emptiness. By choosing to reject the ways of the oppressor and instead pursue peace and justice, we align ourselves with God's will and demonstrate our commitment to living a life that reflects His love and righteousness.

Proverbs 16:29 offers further insight into the destructive influence of the violent man: "A violent man enticeth his neighbor, and leadeth him into the way that is not good." This verse highlights the corrupting effect that the violent man can have on those around him. The violent man is not content to act alone in his aggression; he actively seeks to draw others into his destructive ways. Through manipulation, coercion, or the false promise of power and success, the violent man entices his neighbor, leading him away from the path of righteousness and into behavior that is harmful and morally wrong. The phrase "the way that is not good" underscores the fact that the path of violence is ultimately a path of destruction, both for those who engage in it and for those who are drawn into its influence. In our walk with the Lord, this verse teaches us the importance of being vigilant against the influence of those who seek to lead us away from the values of peace, justice, and love. The violent man's example challenges us to be discerning in our relationships and to resist the temptation to be drawn into conflict or aggression by those who promote such behavior. By standing firm in our commitment to God's principles, we can avoid being led astray by the violent man and remain on the path of righteousness that leads to true peace and fulfillment.

The life of the violent man, as described in these proverbs, serves as a powerful example of the consequences of embracing aggression, coercion, and intimidation as a means to achieve one's goals. His deliberate choice to use violence as a tool for power and control not only harms those around him but also leads to his own moral and spiritual downfall. The violent man's actions are rooted in a desire for dominance and a lack of respect for the inherent dignity and worth of others. His life is marked by conflict, strife, and a deep-seated sense of dissatisfaction, as the pursuit of power through violence ultimately leaves him isolated and spiritually barren. The violent man's story is not just a cautionary tale about the dangers of aggression but also a call to embrace the values of peace, justice, and compassion that are central to a life lived in accordance with God's will.

One of the key lessons we can learn from the violent man is the importance of rejecting the allure of power that comes through violence and intimidation. Proverbs 3:31's warning against envying the oppressor challenges us to examine our own attitudes towards power and success. In a world that often glorifies strength and dominance, it can be tempting to admire those who achieve their goals through force or coercion. However, this verse reminds us that such methods are fundamentally opposed to the values of righteousness and justice that God calls us to uphold. In our walk with the Lord, we must resist the temptation to seek power through violence or aggression and instead strive to live with integrity, compassion, and respect for others. The violent man's example serves as a reminder that true strength lies not in the ability to dominate others but in the ability to act with love and kindness, even in the face of conflict or adversity.

Another important lesson from the violent man is the need to be vigilant against the corrupting influence of those who promote violence and aggression. Proverbs 16:29's depiction of the violent man as someone who entices his neighbor into wrongdoing highlights the danger of being drawn into harmful behavior by others. In our walk with the Lord, we must be discerning in our relationships and careful about the influences we allow into our lives. The violent man's example challenges us to stand firm in our commitment to God's principles, even when others try to lead us astray. By choosing to surround ourselves with those who promote peace, justice, and love, we can protect ourselves from the destructive influence of the violent man and remain on the path of righteousness.

The contrast between the violent man and the values of peace and justice that God calls us to uphold also teaches us about the importance of pursuing reconciliation and understanding in our relationships. The violent man's reliance on force and intimidation creates a cycle of conflict and strife that ultimately leads to destruction. In our walk with the Lord, we must strive to break this cycle by choosing to respond to conflict with humility, patience, and a willingness to seek reconciliation. The violent man's example challenges us to be peacemakers in our communities, working to resolve conflicts through dialogue and understanding rather than through aggression or force. By embracing the values of peace and justice, we can build stronger, healthier relationships and create a more just and compassionate world.

In conclusion, the violent man in Proverbs 3:31 and 16:29 provides us with valuable lessons that are essential for our walk with the Lord. His life serves as a powerful warning of the consequences of embracing aggression, coercion, and intimidation as a means to achieve one's goals. The violent man's deliberate choice to use violence as a tool for power and control not only harms those around him but also leads to his own moral and spiritual downfall. By learning from the violent man's example, we can develop a greater awareness of the dangers of aggression, the importance of rejecting the allure of power that comes through violence, and the need to be vigilant against the corrupting influence of those who promote such behavior. The violent man's story is not just a cautionary tale about the dangers of aggression but also a call to embrace the values of peace, justice, and compassion that are central to a life lived in accordance with God's will. In our walk with the Lord, we must strive to live with integrity, compassion, and respect for others, rejecting the ways of the violent man and choosing instead to be peacemakers in our communities. By doing so, we can create a more just and compassionate world and experience the blessings of a life lived in alignment with God's will. The violent man's life serves as a reminder that the pursuit of power through violence ultimately leads to destruction, and that true strength lies in the ability to act with love and kindness, even in the face of conflict or adversity.

Chapter 20 - Wise in His Own Eyes

Proverbs 26:12, "Seest thou a man wise in his own conceit? There is more hope of a fool than of him," and Proverbs 26:16, "The sluggard is wiser in his own conceit than seven men that can render a reason," provide a sobering and insightful look at the person who is "wise in his own eyes" as described in the book of Proverbs. This individual is characterized by an inflated sense of self-worth, an overestimation of their own knowledge and abilities, and a deep-seated pride that blinds them to their own flaws and the wisdom of others. Unlike the truly wise, who recognize their limitations, seek counsel, and remain open to learning, the person who is wise in their own eyes believes they have all the answers and sees no need for correction or growth. Their life is marked by arrogance, stubbornness, and often a lack of meaningful relationships, as their pride pushes others away. The lessons one can learn from the "wise in his own eyes" figure in Proverbs are crucial for our walk with the Lord, as they teach us about the dangers of pride, the importance of humility, and the value of being teachable and open to the wisdom of others.

Proverbs 26:12 begins with a rhetorical question that draws attention to the problem of self-conceit: "Seest thou a man wise in his own conceit? There is more hope of a fool than of him." This verse highlights the severity of being wise in one's own eyes by stating that even a fool—who is often depicted in Proverbs as someone lacking in judgment and discernment—has more hope than the person who is self-assured in their supposed wisdom. The reason for this harsh comparison is that a fool, though misguided, might still be open to correction and learning. In contrast, someone who is wise in their own eyes is so convinced of their own correctness that they refuse to listen to others, reject feedback, and resist any attempt to guide them onto a better path. Their self-assuredness creates a barrier to growth and improvement because they do not see the need for change. In our walk with the Lord, this verse teaches us the importance of maintaining a humble and teachable spirit. It challenges us to recognize that no matter how much we know or how skilled we become, there is always room for growth and learning. The person who is wise in their own eyes serves as a warning that pride can be a significant obstacle to spiritual and personal development. By acknowledging our limitations and remaining open to the wisdom of others, we can avoid the trap of self-conceit and position ourselves to grow in wisdom and understanding.

Proverbs 26:16 further elaborates on this theme by comparing the self-assuredness of a sluggard with the wisdom of those who can reason: "The sluggard is wiser in his own conceit than seven men that can render a reason." This verse underscores the irrational confidence of someone who is lazy and unmotivated yet still considers themselves wiser than multiple individuals who are capable of sound reasoning and judgment. The sluggard's self-conceit blinds them to the reality of their situation; despite their lack of diligence and effort, they believe they have greater insight than those who have demonstrated their wisdom through thoughtful reasoning. This verse highlights the danger of self-deception, where a person's laziness or lack of effort is masked by a false sense of superiority. In our walk with the Lord, this verse teaches us the importance of not only being diligent and hardworking but also of recognizing the value of others' wisdom. The person who is wise in their own eyes fails to see the benefits of collaboration, counsel, and collective wisdom, which can lead to poor decision-making and missed opportunities for growth. The lesson here is that we should strive to be both humble and industrious, acknowledging that wisdom often comes through the input of others and the willingness to engage in thoughtful reflection and learning. By doing so, we can avoid the pitfalls of arrogance and slothfulness, and instead cultivate a mindset that values effort, collaboration, and continuous improvement.

The life of the person who is wise in their own eyes, as described in these proverbs, serves as a powerful example of the dangers of pride, self-assuredness, and the refusal to acknowledge one's own limitations. Their inflated sense of wisdom and knowledge leads them to dismiss the advice and insights of others, leaving them isolated and often heading down a path of poor decisions and missed opportunities. The person who is wise in their own eyes is not only a danger to themselves but also to those around them, as their stubbornness and arrogance can lead to conflicts, strained relationships, and a lack of progress in both personal and collective endeavors. The lessons we can learn from this figure are essential for understanding the importance of humility, the value of being teachable, and the need to seek out and listen to the wisdom of others.

One of the key lessons we can learn from the person who is wise in their own eyes is the importance of humility in our spiritual and personal growth. Proverbs 26:12's comparison of the self-assured individual with a fool highlights the fact that pride can be a more significant barrier to growth than even foolishness. In our walk with the Lord, we must strive to maintain a humble attitude, recognizing that no matter how much we know or how far we have come, there is always more to learn. The person who is wise in their own eyes serves as a reminder that pride can blind us to our own shortcomings and prevent us from seeing the truth. By embracing humility, we open ourselves up to the possibility of growth, learning from others, and becoming wiser and more effective in our pursuits.

Another important lesson from the person who is wise in their own eyes is the value of being teachable and open to the wisdom of others. Proverbs 26:16's depiction of the sluggard who believes they are wiser than those who can reason underscores the importance of recognizing the limitations of our own understanding. In our walk with the Lord, we must be willing to seek out the counsel and input of others, acknowledging that collective wisdom and thoughtful reasoning often lead to better outcomes than relying solely on our own judgment. The person who is wise in their own eyes fails to see the benefits of collaboration and learning from others, which can lead to poor decision-making and a lack of progress. By cultivating a teachable spirit, we can avoid the pitfalls of self-conceit and instead grow in wisdom, understanding, and effectiveness in all areas of our lives.

The contrast between the person who is wise in their own eyes and those who are truly wise also teaches us about the importance of seeking God's wisdom in all that we do. The self-assured individual relies on their own understanding, often to their detriment, while true wisdom comes from recognizing our dependence on God and seeking His guidance in all aspects of our lives. In our walk with the Lord, we must be careful not to fall into the trap of believing that we have all the answers or that we do not need God's direction. The person who is wise in their own eyes serves as a warning that self-reliance can lead to spiritual and moral blindness, preventing us from seeing the path that God has laid out for us. By continually seeking God's wisdom through prayer, study of His Word, and listening to the counsel of others, we can ensure that we are walking in the truth and making decisions that are aligned with His will.

In conclusion, the person who is wise in their own eyes, as described in Proverbs 26:12 and 26:16, provides us with valuable lessons that are essential for our walk with the Lord. Their life serves as a powerful warning of the dangers of pride, self-assuredness, and the refusal to acknowledge one's own limitations. The inflated sense of wisdom and knowledge that characterizes this individual leads them to dismiss the advice and insights of others, resulting in isolation, poor decision-making, and a lack of meaningful progress. By learning from the example of the person who is wise in their own eyes, we can develop a greater awareness of the importance of humility, the value of being teachable, and the need to seek out and listen to the wisdom of others. The story of the self-assured individual is not just a cautionary tale about the dangers of pride but also a call to embrace humility, recognize our limitations, and seek God's wisdom in all aspects of our lives. In our walk with the Lord, we must strive to maintain a humble and teachable spirit, recognizing that true wisdom comes from acknowledging our dependence on God and being open to learning from others. By doing so, we can avoid the pitfalls of self-conceit and instead grow in wisdom, understanding, and effectiveness in our spiritual journey and in all areas of life. The person who is wise in their own eyes serves as a reminder that true strength lies in humility, and that by seeking God's wisdom and the counsel of others, we can walk in the truth and live a life that is pleasing to Him.

Chapter 21 – The Lustful Man

Proverbs 6:25-29, "Lust not after her beauty in thine heart; neither let her take thee with her eyelids. For by means of a whorish woman a man is brought to a piece of bread: and the adulteress will hunt for the precious life. Can a man take fire in his bosom, and his clothes not be burned? Can one go upon hot coals, and his feet not be burned? So he that goeth in to his neighbor's wife; whosoever toucheth her shall not be innocent," offers a vivid and sobering portrayal of the lustful man as described in the book of Proverbs. The lustful man is characterized by his uncontrolled desires, particularly his sexual lust, which leads him into temptation and ultimately to his downfall. Unlike those who exercise self-control, wisdom, and fidelity, the lustful man allows his desires to dictate his actions, often leading him into morally compromising situations that have severe consequences for his life, relationships, and spiritual well-being. His life is marked by a lack of restraint, a willingness to indulge in fleeting pleasures at the expense of long-term happiness, and a disregard for the moral and ethical boundaries that protect both himself and others. The lessons one can learn from the lustful man in Proverbs are crucial for our walk with the Lord, as they teach us about the dangers of unchecked desires, the importance of self-control, the value of faithfulness, and the need to guard our hearts and minds against the temptations that can lead us away from God's will.

Proverbs 6:25 begins with a direct command: "Lust not after her beauty in thine heart; neither let her take thee with her eyelids." This verse addresses the internal struggle that often precedes external actions, warning against the dangers of allowing lustful thoughts to take root in the heart. The command not to lust after beauty in the heart highlights the importance of controlling our inner desires, as what begins as a seemingly harmless thought can quickly escalate into actions that are morally and spiritually damaging. The reference to being "taken with her eyelids" suggests the subtle yet powerful allure of physical attraction and how easily one can be led astray by focusing on outward appearances rather than on the character and substance of a person. In our walk with the Lord, this verse teaches us the importance of guarding our thoughts and not allowing lust to take hold in our hearts. It challenges us to focus on what is truly important—inner character, integrity, and faithfulness—rather than being swayed by superficial attractions. The lustful man's example serves as a warning that indulging in lustful thoughts can lead to actions that have serious consequences, both for ourselves and for those around us. By maintaining control over our desires and keeping our hearts aligned with God's standards, we can avoid the pitfalls of lust and live a life that honors Him.

Proverbs 6:26-29 further elaborates on the destructive consequences of yielding to lust: "For by means of a whorish woman a man is brought to a piece of bread: and the adulteress will hunt for the precious life. Can a man take fire in his bosom, and his clothes not be burned? Can one go upon hot coals, and his feet not be burned? So he that goeth in to his neighbor's wife; whosoever toucheth her shall not be innocent." These verses use vivid imagery to illustrate the dangers of engaging in illicit relationships, particularly adultery. The phrase "a man is brought to a piece of bread" suggests that giving in to lust can reduce a person to poverty, both materially and spiritually. The pursuit of forbidden pleasure often leads to the loss of one's dignity, reputation, and even livelihood, as the consequences of such actions can be far-reaching and devastating. The verses also emphasize that engaging in sinful relationships is like playing with fire—just as a person cannot carry fire close to their body without getting burned, so too can one not engage in sinful behavior without suffering the consequences. The rhetorical questions about taking fire in one's bosom and walking on hot coals underscore the inevitability of harm when one indulges in lustful actions. In our walk with the Lord, these verses teach us the importance of avoiding situations that can lead to moral compromise. The lustful man's example serves as a reminder that no one is immune to the consequences of sin, and that what may seem like a momentary pleasure can result in long-term pain and suffering. By exercising self-control and setting boundaries that align with God's will, we can protect ourselves from the destructive consequences of lust and maintain our integrity in all areas of life.

The life of the lustful man, as described in these proverbs, serves as a powerful example of the dangers of allowing unchecked desires to control one's actions. His lack of restraint and willingness to indulge in forbidden pleasures lead to a downward spiral of sin, guilt, and ultimately destruction. The lustful man is driven by immediate gratification, often at the expense of his relationships, reputation, and spiritual well-being. His actions not only harm himself but also those around him, as the consequences of his sin ripple out to affect his family, community, and relationship with God. The lustful man's story is not just a cautionary tale about the dangers of sexual sin but also a broader lesson about the importance of self-control, the value of faithfulness, and the need to align our desires with God's will.

One of the key lessons we can learn from the lustful man is the importance of guarding our hearts and minds against temptation. Proverbs 6:25's command not to lust after beauty in the heart challenges us to take control of our thoughts and desires before they lead to sinful actions. In our walk with the Lord, we must be vigilant in monitoring our inner life, recognizing that sin often begins in the heart and mind before it manifests in our behavior. The lustful man's example teaches us that it is not enough to avoid outwardly sinful actions; we must also address the root causes of sin—our thoughts and desires—by bringing them into alignment with God's standards. By cultivating a heart that seeks after righteousness and purity, we can resist the temptations that lead to moral compromise and live a life that reflects God's holiness.

Another important lesson from the lustful man is the need for self-control and the establishment of healthy boundaries. Proverbs 6:26-29's vivid imagery of fire and burning emphasizes the inevitable harm that comes from indulging in sinful behavior. In our walk with the Lord, we must recognize that certain behaviors and situations are inherently dangerous and should be avoided at all costs. The lustful man's example challenges us to set boundaries in our relationships and interactions that protect us from temptation and keep us on the path of righteousness. This includes being mindful of the media we consume, the company we keep, and the situations we place ourselves in, ensuring that we are not exposing ourselves to unnecessary temptation. By exercising self-control and setting boundaries that honor God, we can protect ourselves from the destructive consequences of sin and maintain our integrity in all areas of life.

The contrast between the lustful man and the values of faithfulness and integrity that God calls us to uphold also teaches us about the importance of honoring our commitments, particularly in relationships. The lustful man's pursuit of forbidden pleasure often leads to the breakdown of marriages, families, and communities, as the trust and loyalty that form the foundation of these relationships are undermined by his actions. In our walk with the Lord, we must strive to be faithful in all our relationships, whether in marriage, friendships, or within our community. The lustful man's example serves as a reminder that true fulfillment and happiness are found not in fleeting pleasures but in the deep and lasting bonds that come from living with integrity, faithfulness, and love. By committing to honor our relationships and uphold God's standards of fidelity, we can build a life that is rich in meaningful connections and free from the guilt and shame that accompany moral compromise.

In conclusion, the lustful man in Proverbs 6:25-29 provides us with valuable lessons that are essential for our walk with the Lord. His life serves as a powerful warning of the dangers of allowing unchecked desires to control one's actions, leading to a downward spiral of sin, guilt, and ultimately destruction. The lustful man's lack of restraint and willingness to indulge in forbidden pleasures not only harm himself but also those around him, as the consequences of his actions ripple out to affect his relationships, reputation, and spiritual well-being. By learning from the lustful man's example, we can develop a greater awareness of the importance of guarding our hearts and minds against temptation, exercising self-control, and establishing healthy boundaries in our relationships. The lustful man's story is not just a cautionary tale about the dangers of sexual sin but also a broader lesson about the value of faithfulness, the need to align our desires with God's will, and the importance of living a life that honors Him in all areas. In our walk with the Lord, we must strive to cultivate a heart that seeks after righteousness and purity, set boundaries that protect us from temptation, and commit to honoring our relationships with integrity and faithfulness. By doing so, we can avoid the destructive consequences of lust and build a life that reflects God's holiness, love, and faithfulness. The lustful man's life serves as a reminder that true fulfillment and happiness are found not in fleeting pleasures but in living a life that is aligned with God's will, rooted in His love, and committed to His standards of righteousness.

Chapter 22 – The Deceitful Man

Proverbs 12:5, "The thoughts of the righteous are right: but the counsels of the wicked are deceit," and Proverbs 24:28, "Be not a witness against thy neighbor without cause; and deceive not with thy lips," offer a clear and sobering depiction of the deceitful man as described in the book of Proverbs. The deceitful man is characterized by his willingness to manipulate, lie, and distort the truth for his own gain, often at the expense of others. Unlike those who seek to live righteously, with integrity and honesty, the deceitful man uses deception as a tool to achieve his goals, whether those goals involve personal gain, harm to others, or simply to avoid facing the consequences of his actions. His life is marked by a pattern of dishonesty, manipulation, and betrayal, creating a web of lies that not only entangles those around him but ultimately ensnares him as well. The lessons one can learn from the deceitful man in Proverbs are crucial for our walk with the Lord, as they teach us about the dangers of dishonesty, the importance of living with integrity, the value of truth, and the need to build a life based on trust and righteousness.

Proverbs 12:5 draws a clear distinction between the thoughts of the righteous and the counsels of the wicked: "The thoughts of the righteous are right: but the counsels of the wicked are deceit." This verse emphasizes that the mindset of a righteous person is aligned with truth and justice. The righteous seek to live in a way that is consistent with God's standards, and their thoughts and plans are rooted in honesty, fairness, and a desire to do what is right. In contrast, the wicked, who embody the deceitful man, operate with a mindset that is inherently corrupt. Their counsels, or plans, are based on deceit, manipulation, and lies, with the primary goal of achieving their selfish desires, often at the cost of others' well-being. The deceitful man is driven by a desire to manipulate situations and people to his advantage, regardless of the harm it may cause. In our walk with the Lord, this verse teaches us the importance of aligning our thoughts and actions with God's truth. It challenges us to reject deceit in all its forms, recognizing that any gain achieved through dishonesty is ultimately hollow and destructive. The deceitful man's example serves as a warning that living a life of deception not only damages our relationships with others but also separates us from God, who is the source of all truth and righteousness. By choosing to live with integrity and aligning our thoughts with what is right, we can build a life that reflects God's character and fosters trust and respect in our relationships.

Proverbs 24:28 further underscores the dangers of deceit by admonishing against bearing false witness and using lies to harm others: "Be not a witness against thy neighbor without cause; and deceive not with thy lips." This verse speaks directly to the moral and ethical responsibility we have towards others, particularly in matters of justice and truth. To be a witness against a neighbor without cause means to bring false accusations or to give misleading testimony, actions that can have devastating consequences for the innocent. The verse goes on to warn against using deception in speech, highlighting the destructive power of lies. The deceitful man, by engaging in such behavior, not only harms his neighbor but also undermines the very foundations of trust and justice in his community. In our walk with the Lord, this verse teaches us the importance of honesty and integrity in all our dealings with others. It challenges us to be truthful in our words, to avoid gossip, slander, or any form of deceit that can cause harm to others. The deceitful man's example serves as a stark reminder that lies and deceit may seem to offer a quick solution or a way to gain an advantage, but they ultimately lead to broken relationships, loss of trust, and a damaged reputation. By committing to truthfulness and refusing to participate in deceit, we can build relationships based on trust, foster a sense of justice and fairness, and live in a way that honors God and reflects His righteousness.

The life of the deceitful man, as described in these proverbs, serves as a powerful example of the destructive nature of dishonesty and the importance of living with integrity. His actions, driven by selfishness and a disregard for the truth, create a ripple effect of harm that not only affects those around him but also leads to his own downfall. The deceitful man may achieve temporary success or avoid consequences through his lies, but in the long run, his deceit catches up with him, leading to isolation, loss of trust, and ultimately, judgment. The deceitful man's story is not just a cautionary tale about the dangers of lying and manipulation, but also a call to embrace the values of truth, honesty, and integrity that are central to a life lived in accordance with God's will.

One of the key lessons we can learn from the deceitful man is the importance of aligning our thoughts and actions with truth and integrity. Proverbs 12:5's emphasis on the contrast between the thoughts of the righteous and the deceitful counsels of the wicked challenges us to examine our own motives and actions. In our walk with the Lord, we must strive to cultivate a mindset that is focused on doing what is right, even when it is difficult or inconvenient. The deceitful man's example teaches us that any success achieved through dishonesty is ultimately fleeting and unsatisfying. By committing to a life of integrity, we can build a foundation of trust and respect in our relationships, and ensure that our actions are pleasing to God.

Another important lesson from the deceitful man is the value of truthfulness in our interactions with others. Proverbs 24:28's warning against bearing false witness and using deceitful speech highlights the importance of honesty in maintaining justice and fairness in our communities. In our walk with the Lord, we must be mindful of the impact our words can have on others, and avoid any form of deceit that can cause harm. The deceitful man's example serves as a reminder that lies and manipulation may offer a temporary advantage, but they ultimately lead to broken relationships, loss of trust, and a damaged reputation. By choosing to speak the truth and to act with integrity, we can build strong, healthy relationships that reflect God's love and justice.

The contrast between the deceitful man and the values of truth and integrity that God calls us to uphold also teaches us about the importance of building a life based on trust and righteousness. The deceitful man's actions, rooted in selfishness and a disregard for the truth, lead to a life of isolation and broken relationships. In our walk with the Lord, we must strive to build a life that is grounded in truth and integrity, recognizing that these qualities are essential for maintaining healthy relationships and a strong sense of community. The deceitful man's example challenges us to reject the temptation to use deceit as a tool for personal gain, and instead to embrace the values of honesty, transparency, and fairness that are central to a life lived in accordance with God's will. By doing so, we can build a life that is not only pleasing to God but also rich in meaningful relationships, built on a foundation of trust and mutual respect.

In conclusion, the deceitful man in Proverbs 12:5 and 24:28 provides us with valuable lessons that are essential for our walk with the Lord. His life serves as a powerful warning of the dangers of dishonesty, manipulation, and deceit, and the destructive impact these behaviors can have on our relationships, reputation, and spiritual well-being. The deceitful man's actions, driven by selfishness and a disregard for the truth, not only harm those around him but also lead to his own downfall. By learning from the deceitful man's example, we can develop a greater awareness of the importance of living with integrity, the value of truthfulness in our interactions with others, and the need to build a life based on trust and righteousness. The deceitful man's story is not just a cautionary tale about the dangers of lying and manipulation, but also a call to embrace the values of truth, honesty, and integrity that are central to a life lived in accordance with God's will. In our walk with the Lord, we must strive to cultivate a mindset that is focused on doing what is right, even when it is difficult or inconvenient, and to build a life that reflects God's love and justice. By committing to a life of integrity and truthfulness, we can avoid the pitfalls of deceit and build strong, healthy relationships that are pleasing to God and enriching to our lives. The deceitful man's life serves as a reminder that any gain achieved through dishonesty is ultimately hollow and destructive, and that true fulfillment and success are found in living a life that is aligned with God's will and grounded in the values of truth, integrity, and righteousness.

Chapter 23 – The Proud Man

Proverbs 16:18, "Pride goeth before destruction, and a haughty spirit before a fall," and Proverbs 21:24, "Proud and haughty scorner is his name, who dealeth in proud wrath," provide a compelling and cautionary depiction of the proud man as described in the book of Proverbs. The proud man is characterized by an inflated sense of self-importance, arrogance, and a lack of humility. He is someone who believes he is above others, often disregarding their needs, opinions, and feelings. His life is marked by a sense of superiority that blinds him to his own faults and weaknesses, leading him to make decisions that are ultimately self-destructive. The proud man's arrogance not only alienates him from others but also sets him on a path that leads away from God and towards his own downfall. The lessons one can learn from the proud man in Proverbs are crucial for our walk with the Lord, as they teach us about the dangers of pride, the importance of humility, the value of self-awareness, and the need to align our hearts with God's will.

Proverbs 16:18 offers a timeless truth about the consequences of pride: "Pride goeth before destruction, and a haughty spirit before a fall." This verse underscores the idea that pride is often the precursor to a person's downfall. The proud man, in his arrogance, believes that he is invincible and that his way is always right. He does not see the need to seek counsel, to admit his mistakes, or to learn from others because he is convinced of his own superiority. However, this very attitude leads him to make decisions that are short-sighted, reckless, and ultimately self-destructive. The phrase "haughty spirit" refers to an attitude of disdain or contempt for others, which often accompanies pride. This sense of superiority blinds the proud man to his own vulnerabilities and the potential consequences of his actions, leading him to take risks or make choices that result in his downfall. In our walk with the Lord, this verse teaches us the importance of cultivating humility and being aware of our limitations. It challenges us to recognize that pride can be a significant obstacle to personal growth, healthy relationships, and spiritual development. The proud man's example serves as a warning that an inflated sense of self-worth not only alienates us from others but also sets us on a path that leads to our own destruction. By embracing humility and being open to correction, guidance, and learning from others, we can avoid the pitfalls of pride and live a life that is aligned with God's will and open to His blessings.

Proverbs 21:24 further elaborates on the character of the proud man: "Proud and haughty scorner is his name, who dealeth in proud wrath." This verse highlights the proud man's tendency to not only think highly of himself but also to look down on others with disdain and to react with anger or scorn when his superiority is challenged. The term "scorner" suggests someone who mocks or belittles others, often using sarcasm, criticism, or ridicule to assert his perceived dominance. The proud man's wrath is described as "proud wrath," indicating that his anger is fueled by his pride and sense of entitlement. When things do not go his way or when others fail to recognize his superiority, the proud man reacts with hostility, further alienating himself from those around him. In our walk with the Lord, this verse teaches us the importance of controlling our temper and avoiding the temptation to elevate ourselves at the expense of others. The proud man's example serves as a reminder that anger and scorn are often rooted in pride and can lead to destructive behavior that damages relationships and undermines our witness as followers of Christ. By cultivating a spirit of humility and learning to respond with grace and patience, even in the face of challenges or criticism, we can avoid the trap of proud wrath and build stronger, more positive relationships with others.

The life of the proud man, as described in these proverbs, serves as a powerful example of the dangers of arrogance, self-importance, and a lack of humility. His inflated sense of self-worth leads him to make decisions that are reckless and ultimately self-destructive. The proud man's disdain for others and his tendency to react with anger when his superiority is challenged not only isolate him from meaningful relationships but also lead him further away from God. The proud man's story is not just a cautionary tale about the dangers of pride but also a broader lesson about the importance of humility, self-awareness, and the need to align our hearts with God's will.

One of the key lessons we can learn from the proud man is the importance of cultivating humility in our spiritual and personal lives. Proverbs 16:18's warning that "pride goeth before destruction" challenges us to examine our own attitudes and behaviors, recognizing that an inflated sense of self-worth can lead to our downfall. In our walk with the Lord, we must strive to maintain a humble attitude, recognizing that all we have and all we are comes from God. The proud man's example teaches us that pride can blind us to our own faults and weaknesses, leading us to make decisions that are ultimately harmful to ourselves and others. By embracing humility and being open to correction, guidance, and learning from others, we can avoid the pitfalls of pride and build a life that is aligned with God's will.

Another important lesson from the proud man is the value of self-awareness and the need to control our temper and reactions. Proverbs 21:24's depiction of the proud man as a "scorner" who deals in "proud wrath" highlights the destructive power of pride-fueled anger. In our walk with the Lord, we must be mindful of how our pride can lead us to react negatively to criticism, challenges, or perceived slights. The proud man's example challenges us to develop self-awareness, recognizing when our reactions are driven by pride and learning to respond with grace and humility instead. By controlling our temper and choosing to respond with patience and understanding, we can build stronger relationships and avoid the destructive consequences of proud wrath.

The contrast between the proud man and the values of humility and self-awareness that God calls us to uphold also teaches us about the importance of aligning our hearts with God's will. The proud man's life, marked by arrogance, self-importance, and disdain for others, leads him away from God and towards his own destruction. In our walk with the Lord, we must strive to align our hearts with God's will, recognizing that true strength and wisdom come from humility, not from elevating ourselves above others. The proud man's example serves as a reminder that pride can be a significant obstacle to spiritual growth and that by cultivating humility and self-awareness, we can draw closer to God and experience the fullness of His blessings.

In conclusion, the proud man in Proverbs 16:18 and 21:24 provides us with valuable lessons that are essential for our walk with the Lord. His life serves as a powerful warning of the dangers of pride, arrogance, and a lack of humility. The proud man's inflated sense of self-worth, disdain for others, and tendency to react with anger when his superiority is challenged not only isolate him from meaningful relationships but also lead him further away from God and towards his own destruction. By learning from the proud man's example, we can develop a greater awareness of the importance of humility, self-awareness, and the need to align our hearts with God's will. The proud man's story is not just a cautionary tale about the dangers of pride but also a call to embrace the values of humility, self-awareness, and patience that are central to a life lived in accordance with God's will. In our walk with the Lord, we must strive to maintain a humble attitude, recognizing that all we have and all we are comes from God, and to develop self-awareness that allows us to control our temper and respond to challenges with grace and humility. By doing so, we can avoid the pitfalls of pride and build a life that is aligned with God's will, open to His blessings, and rich in meaningful relationships that reflect His love and grace. The proud man's life serves as a reminder that true strength and wisdom come not from elevating ourselves above others, but from embracing humility, aligning our hearts with God's will, and living a life that honors Him in all we do.

Chapter 24 – The Mocker

Proverbs 21:24, "Proud and haughty scorner is his name, who dealeth in proud wrath," and Proverbs 22:10, "Cast out the scorner, and contention shall go out; yea, strife and reproach shall cease," offer a vivid portrayal of the mocker as described in the book of Proverbs. The mocker is characterized by a prideful and arrogant attitude, one who delights in ridiculing, criticizing, and belittling others. Unlike those who seek wisdom, understanding, and harmony, the mocker thrives on creating discord and conflict through his scornful and dismissive behavior. His life is marked by an unwillingness to listen to others, a tendency to stir up strife, and a profound lack of humility and respect. The mocker often sees himself as above others, taking pleasure in pointing out their flaws and mistakes while refusing to acknowledge his own. The lessons one can learn from the mocker in Proverbs are crucial for our walk with the Lord, as they teach us about the dangers of prideful scorn, the importance of humility, the value of constructive communication, and the need to foster peace and understanding in our relationships.

Proverbs 21:24 begins by describing the mocker with the words "Proud and haughty scorner is his name, who dealeth in proud wrath." This verse highlights the mocker's arrogance and his inclination to deal with others through anger and contempt. The mocker's pride fuels his haughty spirit, leading him to view others as inferior and unworthy of respect. He does not hesitate to express his disdain through scornful remarks, belittling those around him in an attempt to elevate himself. The phrase "proud wrath" indicates that the mocker's anger is not just a reaction to being wronged, but rather an expression of his inflated sense of self-importance. He believes that his opinions and judgments are superior, and anyone who disagrees with him or fails to meet his standards is deserving of his wrath. In our walk with the Lord, this verse teaches us the importance of recognizing and rejecting the attitude of the mocker. It challenges us to examine our own hearts for any traces of pride or haughtiness that might lead us to look down on others or dismiss their perspectives. The mocker's example serves as a warning that dealing with others through scorn and contempt not only damages relationships but also isolates us from the wisdom and growth that come from engaging with others in a spirit of humility and respect. By cultivating a heart of humility and seeking to understand rather than mock, we can build stronger, more positive relationships and reflect the love and grace of God in our interactions with others.

Proverbs 22:10 further emphasizes the disruptive nature of the mocker's behavior: "Cast out the scorner, and contention shall go out; yea, strife and reproach shall cease." This verse suggests that the presence of a mocker in a community or relationship is a source of ongoing conflict and strife. The mocker's scornful attitude and tendency to criticize and belittle others create an environment of tension and hostility, where peace and harmony are constantly undermined. The instruction to "cast out the scorner" indicates that removing such a person from the situation can bring about a cessation of conflict, allowing for the restoration of peace and mutual respect. In our walk with the Lord, this verse teaches us the importance of addressing and confronting scornful behavior in ourselves and others. The mocker's example challenges us to be vigilant in identifying attitudes and actions that contribute to division and discord, and to take steps to promote understanding, cooperation, and reconciliation. By refusing to engage in or tolerate mocking and scornful behavior, we can help create an environment where everyone is valued, and where differences are addressed with respect and empathy rather than with ridicule and contempt.

The life of the mocker, as described in these proverbs, serves as a powerful example of the destructive impact of prideful scorn and the importance of fostering humility, respect, and constructive communication in our relationships. The mocker's arrogance and tendency to ridicule others not only alienate him from meaningful relationships but also contribute to an atmosphere of conflict and division. The mocker's refusal to listen to others, coupled with his eagerness to criticize and belittle, creates a cycle of strife that is difficult to break unless the scornful attitude is addressed and corrected. The mocker's story is not just a cautionary tale about the dangers of pride and scorn but also a broader lesson about the importance of humility, the value of listening and understanding, and the need to promote peace and harmony in our interactions with others.

One of the key lessons we can learn from the mocker is the importance of cultivating humility and avoiding the temptation to look down on others. Proverbs 21:24's description of the mocker as "proud and haughty" challenges us to examine our own attitudes and to guard against any sense of superiority that might lead us to dismiss or ridicule others. In our walk with the Lord, we must strive to approach others with humility, recognizing that we are all made in the image of God and deserving of respect and understanding. The mocker's example teaches us that pride and scorn not only harm our relationships with others but also distance us from the wisdom and growth that come from being open to different perspectives and experiences. By choosing to listen, understand, and engage with others in a spirit of humility and respect, we can build stronger, more meaningful connections and reflect the character of Christ in our interactions.

Another important lesson from the mocker is the value of constructive communication and the importance of addressing conflict in a way that promotes peace and understanding. Proverbs 22:10's instruction to "cast out the scorner" suggests that scornful behavior is a significant barrier to harmony and cooperation. In our walk with the Lord, we must be mindful of how our words and actions can contribute to or detract from the peace and unity of our relationships and communities. The mocker's example challenges us to reject the temptation to criticize, belittle, or ridicule others, and instead to approach conflicts and disagreements with a focus on resolution, understanding, and mutual respect. By promoting constructive communication and being intentional about fostering an environment of respect and empathy, we can help to reduce conflict and create a space where everyone feels valued and heard.

The contrast between the mocker and the values of humility, respect, and peace that God calls us to uphold also teaches us about the importance of aligning our hearts and actions with God's will. The mocker's life, marked by arrogance, scorn, and a desire to elevate himself at the expense of others, leads to conflict, isolation, and a lack of meaningful relationships. In our walk with the Lord, we must strive to align our hearts with God's will, recognizing that true strength and wisdom come from humility, kindness, and a willingness to listen and learn from others. The mocker's example serves as a reminder that scorn and ridicule not only damage our relationships with others but also hinder our spiritual growth and our ability to live out the love and grace that God calls us to demonstrate. By rejecting the ways of the mocker and embracing the values of humility, respect, and peace, we can build a life that is aligned with God's will and that reflects His love and grace in all our interactions.

In conclusion, the mocker in Proverbs 21:24 and 22:10 provides us with valuable lessons that are essential for our walk with the Lord. His life serves as a powerful warning of the dangers of pride, arrogance, and scorn, and the destructive impact these attitudes can have on our relationships and our spiritual well-being. The mocker's prideful and haughty spirit, coupled with his tendency to ridicule and belittle others, not only isolates him from meaningful relationships but also creates an environment of conflict and division. By learning from the mocker's example, we can develop a greater awareness of the importance of humility, respect, and constructive communication, and the need to align our hearts and actions with God's will. The mocker's story is not just a cautionary tale about the dangers of pride and scorn, but also a call to embrace the values of humility, listening, and peace that are central to a life lived in accordance with God's will. In our walk with the Lord, we must strive to cultivate a heart of humility, to approach others with respect and understanding, and to promote peace and harmony in all our relationships. By doing so, we can avoid the pitfalls of pride and scorn, and build a life that is aligned with God's will, open to His blessings, and rich in meaningful relationships that reflect His love and grace. The mocker's life serves as a reminder that true strength and wisdom come not from elevating ourselves above others, but from embracing humility, aligning our hearts with God's will, and living a life that honors Him in all we do.

Chapter 25 – The Contentious Man

Proverbs 26:21, "As coals are to burning coals, and wood to fire; so is a contentious man to kindle strife," provides a vivid and insightful portrayal of the contentious man as described in the book of Proverbs. The contentious man is characterized by his argumentative nature, his tendency to provoke and escalate conflicts, and his apparent desire to stir up discord wherever he goes. Unlike those who seek peace, understanding, and resolution, the contentious man thrives on disagreement and often uses his words and actions to inflame situations rather than to soothe or solve them. His life is marked by constant strife, both in his relationships with others and in his own inner turmoil. The contentious man seems to be driven by a need to assert his own views and opinions, often at the expense of harmony and mutual respect. The lessons one can learn from the contentious man in Proverbs are crucial for our walk with the Lord, as they teach us about the dangers of a quarrelsome spirit, the importance of pursuing peace, the value of constructive communication, and the need to be agents of reconciliation in our relationships.

Proverbs 26:21 uses the imagery of coals and wood feeding a fire to describe the impact of a contentious man on a situation. Just as adding coals to burning coals or wood to a fire causes the fire to grow and intensify, so does the presence of a contentious man in a disagreement or conflict cause the strife to escalate. The contentious man's words and actions act like fuel, making a small disagreement into a larger argument and turning minor issues into major conflicts. Rather than seeking to resolve differences or find common ground, the contentious man appears to take pleasure in keeping the flames of discord burning. His argumentative nature and refusal to back down or compromise only serve to deepen divisions and create an environment of tension and hostility. In our walk with the Lord, this verse teaches us the importance of being peacemakers rather than fire-starters. It challenges us to consider how our words and actions can either contribute to peace or exacerbate conflict. The contentious man's example serves as a warning that a quarrelsome spirit not only damages our relationships with others but also creates an atmosphere of unrest and dissatisfaction in our own lives. By choosing to pursue peace, to listen, and to engage in constructive dialogue, we can avoid the pitfalls of contention and build relationships that are based on mutual respect and understanding.

One of the key lessons we can learn from the contentious man is the importance of self-control, particularly in our speech. The contentious man often speaks without thinking, driven by a desire to prove his point or to win an argument, regardless of the consequences. His words are like the coals and wood that feed the fire of conflict, turning what could be a simple discussion into a heated and destructive argument. In our walk with the Lord, we must be mindful of the power of our words and the impact they can have on others. The contentious man's example challenges us to practice restraint in our speech, to think carefully before we speak, and to consider whether our words will bring peace or add fuel to the fire. By choosing to speak words that are calm, measured, and aimed at resolution rather than escalation, we can help to de-escalate conflicts and foster a more peaceful environment in our relationships and communities.

Another important lesson from the contentious man is the value of humility and the willingness to listen to others. The contentious man is often more concerned with being right than with understanding others' perspectives or finding common ground. His pride and stubbornness prevent him from acknowledging that he might be wrong or that there might be value in others' viewpoints. In our walk with the Lord, we must strive to approach conflicts with humility, recognizing that we do not have all the answers and that others' experiences and perspectives can offer valuable insights. The contentious man's example serves as a reminder that pride and a refusal to listen are major obstacles to resolving conflicts and building healthy relationships. By cultivating a spirit of humility and being willing to listen and learn from others, we can avoid the contentious man's fate and instead become agents of peace and reconciliation.

The life of the contentious man, as described in Proverbs 26:21, also teaches us about the importance of being peacemakers in our communities. The contentious man's constant strife and argumentation create an environment of tension and division, which can have a corrosive effect on relationships and community life. In contrast, those who seek to be peacemakers work to bring people together, to resolve differences, and to create an atmosphere of cooperation and mutual respect. In our walk with the Lord, we are called to be peacemakers, following the example of Christ, who taught that "blessed are the peacemakers, for they shall be called the children of God" (Matthew 5:9). The contentious man's example challenges us to examine how we contribute to the peace and harmony of our communities and to take active steps to promote reconciliation, understanding, and cooperation. By choosing to be peacemakers, we can help to build communities that reflect God's love and grace, where differences are addressed with respect and understanding rather than with anger and division.

The contrast between the contentious man and the values of peace, humility, and constructive communication that God calls us to uphold also teaches us about the importance of aligning our hearts and actions with God's will. The contentious man's life, marked by constant strife and conflict, leads to broken relationships, isolation, and a lack of inner peace. In our walk with the Lord, we must strive to align our hearts with God's will, recognizing that true peace and fulfillment come from living in harmony with others and seeking to resolve conflicts in a way that honors God. The contentious man's example serves as a reminder that a quarrelsome spirit not only harms our relationships with others but also disrupts our own peace of mind and spiritual well-being. By rejecting the ways of the contentious man and embracing the values of peace, humility, and reconciliation, we can build a life that is aligned with God's will and that reflects His love and grace in all our interactions.

In conclusion, the contentious man in Proverbs 26:21 provides us with valuable lessons that are essential for our walk with the Lord. His life serves as a powerful warning of the dangers of a quarrelsome spirit, the destructive impact of constant strife, and the importance of pursuing peace, humility, and constructive communication in our relationships. The contentious man's argumentative nature, refusal to back down, and tendency to escalate conflicts not only damage his relationships with others but also create an atmosphere of tension and division that is harmful to both himself and those around him. By learning from the contentious man's example, we can develop a greater awareness of the importance of self-control in our speech, the value of humility and the willingness to listen, and the need to be peacemakers in our communities. The contentious man's story is not just a cautionary tale about the dangers of constant strife but also a call to embrace the values of peace, humility, and reconciliation that are central to a life lived in accordance with God's will. In our walk with the Lord, we must strive to cultivate a heart of peace, to approach conflicts with humility and a desire to understand, and to promote reconciliation and cooperation in all our relationships. By doing so, we can avoid the pitfalls of contention and build a life that is aligned with God's will, open to His blessings, and rich in meaningful relationships that reflect His love and grace. The contentious man's life serves as a reminder that true strength and wisdom come not from winning arguments or proving ourselves right, but from embracing humility, aligning our hearts with God's will, and living a life that honors Him in all we do.

Chapter 26 – The Faithless Man

Proverbs 2:22, "But the wicked shall be cut off from the earth, and the transgressors shall be rooted out of it," and Proverbs 21:8, "The way of man is froward and strange: but as for the pure, his work is right," provide a profound and cautionary depiction of the faithless man as described in the book of Proverbs. The faithless man is characterized by his lack of commitment to God, his tendency to walk in disobedience, and his refusal to live by the principles of righteousness. Unlike those who seek to follow God's path with integrity and faith, the faithless man chooses a path of rebellion, dishonesty, and moral compromise. His life is marked by a disregard for spiritual truth, a pursuit of selfish desires, and an inclination to deviate from the righteous way. The faithless man's actions not only lead to his own downfall but also bring harm to others and contribute to the decay of moral and spiritual values in the broader community. The lessons one can learn from the faithless man in Proverbs are crucial for our walk with the Lord, as they teach us about the dangers of spiritual compromise, the importance of faithfulness, the value of living a life of integrity, and the need to remain steadfast in our commitment to God.

Proverbs 2:22 offers a stark warning about the ultimate fate of the wicked and faithless: "But the wicked shall be cut off from the earth, and the transgressors shall be rooted out of it." This verse emphasizes the inevitable consequences of living a life that is disconnected from God and His principles. The faithless man, who chooses to walk in wickedness and transgression, is warned that his actions will lead to his being "cut off" and "rooted out," symbolizing complete and utter removal from the blessings and life that God offers to those who walk in righteousness. The imagery of being "cut off" and "rooted out" suggests that the faithless man's life is unsustainable and destined for destruction because it is not grounded in the truth and stability that come from a relationship with God. In our walk with the Lord, this verse teaches us the importance of remaining rooted in God's Word and His ways. It challenges us to examine our own lives and to ensure that we are not allowing ourselves to be led astray by the temptations and deceptions of the world. The faithless man's example serves as a warning that spiritual compromise and disobedience have serious consequences, not only in this life but also in the life to come. By choosing to remain faithful to God, to walk in His ways, and to reject the path of the faithless, we can secure our place in the life and blessings that God has prepared for those who love Him.

Proverbs 21:8 further illustrates the contrast between the way of the faithless man and the way of the righteous: "The way of man is froward and strange: but as for the pure, his work is right." This verse highlights the twisted and morally corrupt nature of the faithless man's path. The term "froward" refers to a stubborn and perverse attitude, indicating that the faithless man's way is not only crooked but also deliberately resistant to correction and guidance. The word "strange" suggests that the faithless man's behavior is out of alignment with what is good, right, and natural according to God's standards. In contrast, the work of the pure—the one who is faithful and committed to God—is described as "right," meaning that it is upright, just, and in harmony with God's will. The faithless man's refusal to walk in righteousness leads him down a path that is morally distorted and ultimately self-destructive. In our walk with the Lord, this verse teaches us the importance of choosing the path of righteousness and rejecting the ways of the faithless. The faithless man's example challenges us to resist the temptations of moral compromise and to remain steadfast in our commitment to doing what is right, even when it is difficult or unpopular. By aligning our actions with God's standards and choosing to walk in purity and integrity, we can avoid the pitfalls of the faithless man and live a life that is pleasing to God.

The life of the faithless man, as described in Proverbs 2:22 and 21:8, serves as a powerful example of the dangers of spiritual compromise, disobedience, and a lack of faith. His refusal to live by the principles of righteousness and his willingness to walk in wickedness lead to his ultimate downfall and destruction. The faithless man's actions not only harm himself but also contribute to the moral and spiritual decay of the community around him. His life is marked by a pattern of dishonesty, moral compromise, and a disregard for the truth, which ultimately leads to his being "cut off" and "rooted out" from the blessings that God offers to those who walk in His ways. The faithless man's story is not just a cautionary tale about the dangers of spiritual disobedience but also a broader lesson about the importance of faithfulness, integrity, and the need to remain committed to God's path in all areas of life.

One of the key lessons we can learn from the faithless man is the importance of remaining faithful to God and His principles, even in the face of temptation and challenges. Proverbs 2:22's warning that the wicked and transgressors will be "cut off" and "rooted out" challenges us to examine our own lives and to ensure that we are not allowing ourselves to be led astray by the deceptions and distractions of the world. In our walk with the Lord, we must strive to remain rooted in God's Word, to walk in obedience to His commands, and to reject the path of the faithless, which leads to destruction. The faithless man's example teaches us that spiritual compromise and disobedience have serious consequences, and that true fulfillment and security are found in a life that is grounded in faithfulness to God.

Another important lesson from the faithless man is the value of living a life of integrity and righteousness. Proverbs 21:8's contrast between the "froward and strange" way of the faithless man and the "right" work of the pure highlights the importance of choosing to walk in righteousness, even when it is difficult or unpopular. In our walk with the Lord, we must be mindful of the choices we make and the paths we choose, ensuring that they are in alignment with God's standards and His will. The faithless man's example challenges us to resist the temptations of moral compromise and to remain steadfast in our commitment to doing what is right. By choosing to live a life of integrity and righteousness, we can avoid the pitfalls of the faithless man and live a life that is pleasing to God and in harmony with His purposes.

The contrast between the faithless man and the values of faithfulness, integrity, and righteousness that God calls us to uphold also teaches us about the importance of aligning our hearts and actions with God's will. The faithless man's life, marked by spiritual compromise, disobedience, and moral corruption, leads to his ultimate destruction and separation from the blessings of God. In our walk with the Lord, we must strive to align our hearts with God's will, recognizing that true strength and wisdom come from a life of faithfulness, obedience, and commitment to God's path. The faithless man's example serves as a reminder that spiritual compromise not only harms our relationship with God but also jeopardizes our eternal destiny. By rejecting the ways of the faithless man and embracing the values of faithfulness, integrity, and righteousness, we can build a life that is aligned with God's will, open to His blessings, and secure in His promises.

In conclusion, the faithless man in Proverbs 2:22 and 21:8 provides us with valuable lessons that are essential for our walk with the Lord. His life serves as a powerful warning of the dangers of spiritual compromise, disobedience, and a lack of faith, and the destructive impact these behaviors can have on our relationship with God and our eternal destiny. The faithless man's refusal to live by the principles of righteousness and his willingness to walk in wickedness lead to his ultimate downfall and destruction, as he is "cut off" and "rooted out" from the blessings that God offers to those who walk in His ways. By learning from the faithless man's example, we can develop a greater awareness of the importance of remaining faithful to God, the value of living a life of integrity and righteousness, and the need to align our hearts and actions with God's will. The faithless man's story is not just a cautionary tale about the dangers of spiritual disobedience but also a call to embrace the values of faithfulness, integrity, and righteousness that are central to a life lived in accordance with God's will. In our walk with the Lord, we must strive to remain rooted in God's Word, to walk in obedience to His commands, and to reject the path of the faithless, which leads to destruction. By doing so, we can avoid the pitfalls of the faithless man and build a life that is aligned with God's will, open to His blessings, and secure in His promises. The faithless man's life serves as a reminder that true fulfillment and security are found not in moral compromise or disobedience, but in a life that is grounded in faithfulness to God, committed to His path, and lived in accordance with His principles.

Conclusion

As we conclude "Proverbs' Portraits - The Men God Mentions", it's clear that the lessons found in the book of Proverbs are as powerful and relevant today as they were when they were first written. Through our exploration of the various men God highlights in Proverbs, we've seen how the choices these men made—whether wise or foolish—shaped their lives and impacted those around them. The portraits of these men serve as both warnings and examples, urging us to reflect on our own paths and the kind of men or women we are becoming. Whether it's the wisdom of the prudent man, the diligence of the hardworking man, or the humility of the righteous man, these qualities shine as beacons of light, guiding us toward a life that honors God and brings about lasting peace and joy. On the other hand, the foolishness of the lazy man, the deceit of the dishonest man, and the pride of the arrogant man remind us of the dangers that come with straying from God's ways. They show us how easily one can fall into traps of selfishness, greed, and anger, leading to a life filled with regret and sorrow. As we've studied these men, we've also been reminded of God's desire for us to choose wisdom, to walk in His truth, and to live lives marked by integrity and faithfulness. The book of Proverbs is more than just a collection of sayings; it's a guidebook for life, offering us the wisdom we need to navigate the challenges we face and the choices we must make. As we close this book, let's carry with us the lessons we've learned from the men God mentions. Let's strive to embody the characteristics of the wise, the diligent, and the righteous, while avoiding the pitfalls of the foolish, the lazy, and the prideful. In a world filled with distractions and temptations, may we remain steadfast in our pursuit of wisdom and righteousness, always seeking to honor God in all we do. "Proverbs' Portraits - The Men God Mentions" serves as a reminder that God sees our actions, knows our hearts, and calls us to live lives that reflect His goodness and truth. As we move forward, may we continue to learn from the wisdom of Proverbs, letting it shape our decisions, guide our actions, and inspire us to be the kind of people God desires us to be—people who are wise, faithful, and true, shining His light in a world that desperately needs it.

Don't miss out!

Visit the website below and you can sign up to receive emails whenever Joshua Rhoades publishes a new book. There's no charge and no obligation.

https://books2read.com/r/B-A-AJLBB-TMHYE

BOOKS2READ

Connecting independent readers to independent writers.

Did you love *Proverbs' Portraits The Men God Mentions*? Then you should read *Sounding The Call - The Voice of Conviction*[1] by Joshua Rhoades!

[2]

In a world filled with noise, where countless voices vie for our attention, the voice of conviction often stands out as a beacon of truth and clarity. This voice, rooted in the divine call to righteousness, echoes through the ages, urging humanity to confront sin, seek justice, and return to a life aligned with God's will. Isaiah 58:1 captures this urgency and powerfully encapsulates the role of the prophet: "Cry aloud, spare not, lift up thy voice like a trumpet, and shew my people their transgression, and the house of Jacob their sins." This verse is not merely a relic of ancient scripture but a timeless call that remains profoundly relevant today.

---

1. https://books2read.com/u/ba5XVy

2. https://books2read.com/u/ba5XVy

"Sounding The Call - The Voice of Conviction" is a deep exploration of Isaiah 58:1, its significance, and its pressing relevance for our contemporary world. This book looks into the heart of the prophet's mandate, examining the imperative to speak out against wrongdoing, to call out injustice, and to urge communities back to the path of righteousness. In an era where moral relativism often blurs the lines between right and wrong, the clarion call of Isaiah 58:1 reminds us of the unchanging standards of God's truth and the necessity of upholding them with courage and conviction.

Today, as in the days of Isaiah, the world is in desperate need of voices that are unafraid to speak the truth. The command to "cry aloud" is not just for the prophets of old; it is a charge to every believer to lift their voice against the injustices and sins that plague our societies. Whether it is addressing the deep-seated issues of inequality, corruption, or moral decay, the message of Isaiah 58:1 is a powerful reminder that silence is not an option when faced with evil. The call to "spare not" emphasizes the need for unwavering commitment to truth, even when it is inconvenient or unpopular. It challenges us to confront our own complacency and to take an active stand in the face of wrongdoing.

This book also explores the metaphor of the trumpet used in Isaiah 58:1—a symbol of urgency, clarity, and the need to capture attention. Just as a trumpet blast cuts through the noise, the voice of conviction must be bold and clear, leaving no room for ambiguity. In a time when many are reluctant to speak out for fear of criticism or backlash, "Sounding The Call" encourages readers to embrace their role as bearers of truth, to lift their voices without fear, and to stand firm in their convictions.

"Sounding The Call - The Voice of Conviction" is not just an exposition of Isaiah 58:1; it is a call to action. It invites readers to reflect on the relevance of this ancient text in their own lives and to consider how they can be voices of conviction in their communities. In exploring the need for prophetic voices today, this book challenges each of us to examine our own response to the injustices we see around us and to be willing to "cry aloud" in the pursuit of righteousness.

As you journey through these pages, may you be inspired to listen to the voice of conviction within you, to boldly proclaim the truth, and to live out the call of Isaiah 58:1 in a world that desperately needs it. The time to sound the call is now. The voice of conviction is yours to lift.